Stop Complaining

Guide to Living Life Instead of Complaining About It

Published June 2009, Russellville, KY USA

ISBN: 978-0-557-12383-4

Dedication:

To my beautiful husband, sons, mother-in-law, and animals that remind me always to be thankful.

Table of Contents

About the Author   7

Chapter 1   9

unproductive Complaining

Chapter 2   45

taking Ownership

Chapter 3   59

verbal Complaints

Chapter 4   85

redirecting Energy

Chapter 5 105

the right to be Happy

Chapter 6 125

accepting Change

Chapter 7 141

just say Thank You

Chapter 8 161

breaking the Habit

Chapter 9 173

justified Complaining

Chapter 10 187

taking Action

About the Author

Author Meilena Hauslendale began her career at a very young age working as a journalist, freelancer and contributing author. In 1997, Meilena embarked on her career as an inspirational artist, initially developing her style by displaying her art along with inspirational sayings. Her work was then featured internationally through galleries and publications. It wasn't until 2002 that she began publishing her writing in the form of personal development articles and books.

She is the author of *Making Your Purpose Your Business, Recognizing Unhealthy Relationships, The Spiritual Revolution, Natural Parenting: Guide to Pregnancy, Birth, & Beyond,* and *Onward Rising – A Memoir.*

The unique combination of art and literature has drawn recognition from both the art and writing community. In 2004, she was inducted into **Who's**

Who of American Women for 2004-2005, the definitive biographical resource featuring the most accomplished women in all areas of human endeavor.

To read more about Meilena, please visit us at:

http://www.imotivate.org

and

http://www.meilena.com

Chapter 1

unproductive COMPLAINING

The average person complains 20 times a day.[31] If we multiply this number times the number of people living in the world, 6,635,544,887, we would average 132,710,897,740 complaints in a 24-hour period. How many of these complaints are actually valid and how many complaints are not? Granted, some complaints are valid forms of criticism, but there are also a large majority of complaints that are quite unnecessary. Complaints of this nature become a form of negativity that can spread rapidly among a group of people.

Complaints, unfortunately, are not isolated to the complainer alone. A complaint is usually not kept

---

[1] According to the Creator of the Complaint Free World By Will Bowen

to oneself; instead it is told to another person or to groups of people, which therefore can lead to other complainers. A complaint can actually "seed" itself into the thoughts of others.

According to Dictionary.com, the definition of complaint is as follows:

com·plaint(kom-plānt') n.
1. An expression of pain, dissatisfaction, or resentment.

It is not that complaining is "wrong" or not constructive, as this form of criticism can mark changes on the world to make it a better place. However, *unproductive* complaining can lead to a negative outlook on life and one's surroundings.

Let's face it, complaining is time-consuming. We can spend hours just trying to convince someone to validate our claims of discomfort and then not take any action to change or better our situation. What happens is we waste very valuable time and don't even work to make or create a difference.

When we make mistakes in our lives we have two options. We can choose to recover from the situation and make amends to the persons we have harmed, or we can simply complain, and force blame onto other people for our own actions and choices.

In life, we can identify with getting a simple cut on our finger. We can choose to take two forms of action: we can either take care of the injury and put a band-aid on it to heal, or we can leave it alone and continue to let it fester and worsen.

Perhaps changing our views on complaints will help us look at what crucial roles they can have in our lives and how much control a complaint can initially have to not only ourselves but to those around us.

It's okay to express our thoughts to people we love and to the people we have to interact with, as this is a part of our own communication and growth. However, it is important to choose our battles wisely, as this allows us to differentiate responsibilities that we own from responsibilities that we don't own.

For example, let's say there is a married man who is abused by his wife. We will say she is an abusive alcoholic who becomes disruptive during drunkenness. The man complains to a close friend about the situation he faces daily with this woman. He tells his friend of all the horrible things that she does and how she is taking his money while he is working.

The friend agrees this behavior is not good and that he doesn't deserve to be treated this way. The conversation ends. The man returns to his friend the following day and continues to describe another event that took place with his wife being abusive, same complaints, just a different day.

The complainer continues to describe the situation to his confidant, but never takes any action to find a solution that suits his needs and betters his environment. Instead, what happens in this particular example is that the person begins to deteriorate within his own world. He becomes isolated by the problem instead of freed by the solution.

Another example: let's say we have a woman who is severely beaten by her boyfriend on a weekly basis. She confides in a close friend. She admits that the relationship is harming her, but never takes any action to get her out of this threatening situation. Instead, she returns to the relationship and starts the unhealthy cycle all over again. She continues to return to her friend and continues to complain, but never follows up on her own grievances.

Both of these examples are of "unproductive" complaining. It is not that the man and woman in our examples did not have a valid reason to complain, because they certainly did. It is the fact that they did not take any actions with their complaints and work towards a solution to their problems. Instead, they continued to make a wrong-doing unto them and had involved innocent bystanders in the process: the confidants, their family, and anyone else directly associated with them.

We are responsible for our own happiness and well-being. It is up to us to identify what is beneficial to our situations in life and what is not beneficial to us. We are either taking care of ourselves and the loved ones around us, or we are choosing to be oblivious and unaware. We will either work towards our goals and find solutions to our problems, or we will simply wade in the waters of complacency, and take no action at all.

There are abusive situations like the ones in our examples that occur daily. Some, however, are even more extreme and brutal. Some life situations like this even result in death. No matter how big or small a complaint may be, all complaints that we have in our lives should be properly assessed. Consider small complaints to be practice for larger-scaled complaints.

Complaints without action can lead to a destructive consequence. Choose your battles wisely. If you have the power to control a situation by your reaction alone then take the time to think the situation through and make a positive choice for change. Weigh out your options. Talk to someone you trust or better yet write out your thoughts and make two columns so you can clearly see the pros and the cons of an issue.

Whether the complaint is big or small, we should still give ourselves the same respect that we would give a friend in a similar situation. We still need to devote our attention to an ultimate solution to help satisfy our complaint. Sometimes this may mean finding a compromise, a middle ground that satisfies both parties involved, or sometimes this even means abandoning the situation altogether and starting over.

Change begins with us. When we voice our opinions or our complaints to others, we are essentially trying to organize our own thoughts verbally. This can be a very therapeutic form of communication to ourselves without us even realizing to what extent of purpose that it serves.

We can have several thoughts pass through our head in one minute alone.

[2]*According to the National Science Foundation, the average person thinks about 12,000 thoughts per day while awake. Deep thinkers have as many as 50,000 thoughts per day.*

---

[2] National Science Foundation- http://www.nsf.gov/

Now that we have an idea of how many thoughts may pass through our minds in a day, we can understand why it could be difficult for us to manage all the information that we receive and take action on even half of it without organization.

Also, we have to consider out of the number of thoughts that go through our minds, what percentage of these thoughts are positive and what percentage of these thoughts are negative? How many of these thoughts that we have result in our own formulation of complaints, which are ultimately expressions of our own dissatisfaction?

When we communicate to another person our particular thoughts, we are filing the information in our heads like a mental filing cabinet. We are saving these details for later. Not only are we filing away the actual situation, but we are also filing away the context in which we shared our thoughts with other people on the matter.

Sharing our personal life details to someo[ne we] trust can allow us to verbalize our emotions. [We put] the pieces of our puzzle out there for someone else to see and it forces us to share the details and to create a sequence of events. This process forces us to organize our ideas and also voice our opinions about the situation that is affecting us.

Whereas on the inside of our own person, we may feel scattered and unclear on what viable solutions exist due to confusion. This is comparable to us sitting in a cluttered room and trying to find something. We can't see what it is we are looking for because there is no organization. There is no order or path cleared out for us to determine a direction. Having this mental clutter can result in us standing still instead of taking action. Clutter can overwhelm someone to the point of exhaustion. Mental clutter can affect us in the same way, leaving us feel too overwhelmed to take action because we can't seem to find out where to start or begin.

Whereas, if we dropped something in an empty room, we are able to see where it went and retrieve it almost instantly. The same concept can be applied to our thoughts and our emotions.

Extracting our inner feelings and placing them out there in the open to another person helps us clean up what we have in our head. This also allows us to isolate our thoughts for a moment simply by sharing them with someone else. When we verbalize our thoughts about a situation to someone, we are releasing the power they tend to have over us. This is very much like a mental detoxification where we are draining something out of us that has taken hostage of our thoughts. We are giving our thoughts freedom by allowing them to surface instead of trying to ignore them.

Sharing our emotions and getting our complaints out there in the open is important; however, we also need to make a wise choice as to whom we share our feelings with and whom we complain to. Not all people will attribute to making a positive decision for you. We must always remember that no matter what, we are in control of our choices. We are in control of the actions that we choose to execute. So take notice with whom you want to share these intimate thoughts.

Sometimes you can choose the wrong person to voice your situations to and what might occur is that instead of feeling better about the situation, you are only left with even more doubts and concerns. Or worse yet, you can be led in a direction that someone else thought was right for you versus something you felt was right for yourself. We have to base our decisions on our own instincts and not the instincts or opinions of others.

Did you ever have someone that you could talk to and trust? After you were done speaking with them, you always felt hopeful afterwards. This is a perfect example of how you should feel after you speak with the right person. Instead of feeling foggy and cloudy, you should feel like a weight was lifted off of your shoulders and your inner burden was divided in half.

It is important that you store your feelings with this friend into memory as this will allow you to compare future encounters with others and help decipher positive versus negative friendships. There are friendships that add to our well-being and friendships that take away from our well-being. It is important that we remember both.

If you speak to someone and disclose your feelings and do not feel resolved or are left feeling more confused then one of two issues may have occurred. The first issue might be that you have not contemplated your complaint and the validity of your own dissatisfaction to make a pure judgment. The second issue could be that you chose to share your emotions with someone that is not capable of understanding them in the first place. In other words, you went to someone who did not have the tools or experience of contributing to understand your situation.

This can be quite common with family. It is easy to assume because you are "family" that these people should understand who you are as a person. It is easy to assume that the people that have known you all your life and have been the primary influence for your pre-adult decisions should want to listen to you, and should be helpful. This is not always the case at all though, especially if you come from a family that stems from dysfunction and unhealthy behaviors.

It is important for us to always look at the "source" and evaluate whom we share our feelings with. Are we going to a person that has issues handling their own life situations? If we are sharing our deepest thoughts with someone that has trouble dealing with their own daily life issues, then we are not likely going to receive a positive solution or outlook from this person. We may even end up receiving information that we could do without, not to mention increased confusion.

Family opinions of you or your situation can vary heavily. Often what happens is that their opinions of you are tainted forms of information that can be more harmful than positive as they have a different idea of what your life should be versus the picture of life you want for yourself. So be very careful when you attempt to complain or share your inner thoughts with people you think are 'close' to you, as they may not want to see the 'real' you. Family can put blinders on and narrow their own views by sometimes only seeing one side of the story or they may isolate you in a time frame that they felt comfortable with and that is often your childhood. As we evolve, our opinions and life situations change, even though family members may not always see us in that light.

Sometimes the closest person to you can be someone outside the immediate "family" realm. Maybe you have a spouse that you can tell anything to and always feel acknowledged and clear-headed afterwards. Maybe you have a friend that you made over the years that always had a lot to offer you in the form of comfort and communication.

Our lives make up for whatever we lack. If we lack family support then we are provided a close friend or confidant that we can share our experiences with. The universe never leaves us without unless that is where we are intended to be for a moment, but we are always provided with gifts in the form of people. We are given the right person when it is needed. There is a Buddhist proverb that says, "When the student is ready, the teacher will appear."

If we pay attention to life events and reflect on the people that were brought into our lives during those times, if we acted on our instincts and our guts, we were often led to the appropriate people at the perfect time. When we were ready to learn there was someone there to listen and someone there to teach us, and to help us move forward… evolve.

Outside people can be the most beautiful gifts of validity that you could ever imagine because they are distanced from you and the situations that you have encountered. They don't know our backgrounds or our roots. They don't have our lives isolated in time because they only are now learning who we are. There is no preconceived notion. The slate we have is clear with them and not hindered by what someone else told them about us.

We actually have the opportunity to explain ourselves as we see fit. We have the right to present ourselves to someone in a way that we would like to be looked at, not in the way that someone else viewed us.

A perfect example is someone that may have grown up in a disruptive family that has unhealthy interactions with one another. If they wanted to perhaps complain about someone within the family to another family member, they might not get a response of the truest form. Family members can be biased with their opinions that they provide. Instead of being neutral like a therapist, they can be very opinionated on the issue as it may hit too close to "home."

Some family members don't want conflicts to be out in the open. They feel that a conflict is resolved when it is no longer discussed. They would rather cover the issue up than deal with its reality. So when you address inner family issues with another family member instead of responding appropriately to your pleas, they might try to convince you to not address the issue and just move past it. Instead of correcting this issue, they may advise you to just avoid it altogether.

Avoiding an issue can sometimes cause more harm than good. Part of our own awareness in life allows us the responsibility to help others become aware of their actions whether they are positive or negative. Instead of being a part of the problem and enabling someone to stay in a pattern, we have the opportunity to address an issue and bring it into reality. We will find that not only are we forcing ourselves to be honest, but we are also presenting the truth to others around us, which will have its own impact on the situation.

If you went to your spouse, who was your best friend, they would help you to see the injustices or truths within your family. They would likely provide you with a different perspective than the family member, as they have not grown up with the immunity to family issues like you have. Your spouse or your closest friend might be able to see the finer details that you may have overlooked simply because of their lack of exposure to your family environment. They are able to provide you with a different perspective and perhaps validate claims that you were aware of but afraid to address.

They can do so because they are distant from the subject matter and the people involved. They don't have a history with your family like you do. They are not biased out of loyalty to your family. They don't care if they say something truthful yet offensive because they are removed from the situation. This person, whether it is a spouse or a close confidant, is the ideal person to share your feelings with because you are going to very likely receive a different perspective than you would dealing with someone too close to the issue at hand.

Granted, some families are very close and you may have someone that you can confide in and trust within your family circle, and that is fine as well. Just choose your confidants wisely like you would choose a juror for the court. You want to always make sure you are speaking with someone that acknowledges your issue in a neutral manner.

When we are choosing a confidant there are several points to consider. We can assess the people we trust and are involved with. We can assess current confidants based on these characteristics to see if we are confiding in people with our best interest at heart:

1. Don't talk about a situation with someone that may have a biased opinion.
2. Always keep in mind that no matter who you share your inner complaints with, you have control of the final action.
3. If you don't want someone's opinion then don't ask for it.
4. Organize your own thoughts first before sharing them with others.

Trusting others can come easily for some people and for others, they have a reason to be skeptical. In this day and age, good and honest people are very hard to come by. So it is important that we be careful with our words and be careful with whom we share our own truths with. Not everyone has our best interest at heart, not even people we may "think" are close to us.

With our first rule, we state "Don't talk about a situation with someone that may have a biased opinion." If you are going to share your feelings and try to work out a plan of action, don't speak with a person that may be biased with the outcome.

For example, if you are having issues with a relationship and you are not sure that you want to continue the relationship, then don't go to your partner's closest friend to discuss your concerns. Obviously they will have your partner's interest at heart or even worse, have an ulterior motive that you may or may not be aware of.

Our second rule is "Always keep in mind that no matter whom you share your inner complaints with, you have control of the final action." No matter what someone tells you to do in regards to your situation, in the end, you are the only one that can take action. You do not have to take someone's opinion and turn it into an action. You have the power and the ability to make your own choices even if someone may disagree with them. Be aware that when you are speaking with someone about your situation or issue, you will get responses that you may not feel are appropriate for you. You have the ability to decipher what is beneficial to you and your issue.

You can quietly say, "Thanks for your opinion" and leave it at that if you disagree with the advice given. You don't have to explain why you oppose their advice. You don't have to even give details for your own actions. All you have to know is that you have the ability to make a choice and educate yourself on positive choices to make. What is right for one person may not be right for another person. That is why it is crucial that we assess our own situations wisely instead of allowing others to make choices for us.

Our third guideline is "If you don't want someone's opinion then don't ask for it." If you know there is someone that you communicate with on a daily basis that has different ideas on what your life should be, then don't bother wasting your time or energy on telling them your situation, as the results will likely always be the opposite of what you think they should be. We are simply wasting our breath in telling someone that we know will disagree with us, as this will only yield the same negative results.

So in order to avoid conflict, bypass sharing your thoughts with people that you didn't want their opinions in the first place. It will make your life a little less confusing to not include them on your personal endeavors and a lot more peaceful too. Remember you do not have to convince disbelievers of you, nor argue and spend time trying to achieve the unachievable. Everyone has an opinion and it is not our job to make sure someone else's opinion matches our own.

With our fourth rule, "Organize your own thoughts first before sharing them with others." When we don't have our own thoughts organized, we tend to be vulnerable to the thoughts and opinions others may leave behind. To prevent us from being susceptible to this occurrence, take time out to sort your thoughts wisely. If you don't have the answer for you situation, be patient and realize that it will soon come. More information will always be revealed.

Sometimes we rush towards others all too quickly in hope of instant gratification, when instead, this can lead to more confusion. If you have an idea of what you want the outcome to be, then all you need to do is visualize how to achieve this. What is right for one may not be what is right for you. So even if someone has intentions of rescuing you and coming to your aid, ultimately, only you can determine what your intuition is telling you.

In the midst of chaos and confusion, realize that it is all right to take moments of silence to get your feelings sorted out before conveying them to others. It is during these moments we gain the confidence that we need to address what types of emotions we are having.

We can say we are angry. We can say we are sad. We can admit that we don't know right now what we feel. Instead of someone else stepping in and telling us how we should feel or what we feel, we are allowing ourselves that time to identify our own feelings and take ownership of them.

It's okay to step back and look at the situation from a different angle. We can stop and look at ourselves, the situation we are in, and the direction that we want to take. Even if we are under a time constraint, we can still stop for a few minutes or hours to evaluate ourselves and the situation we are approaching.

Taking these moments to reflect can be crucial, as these moments are allowing us to create our own identity without us even realizing it. We are given obstacles in life so that we can practice our skills, our balance, and our focus. Everyone needs practice. A professional baseball player is only good at what they do because they took the time to perfect their game. Life is no different. We have to take the time to look at the bigger picture. Every situation we encounter in our lives, whether big or small, is not an opportunity for us to complain; it is an opportunity for us to learn and grow.

Do we always like the lessons? No, but that is often because we don't understand their purpose or intentions in our lives. If we look at the bigger picture, we can understand that our hardships may have a deeper meaning than what we can imagine. Every situation we encounter in life allows us to make a choice. Sometimes we make good decisions and sometimes we don't. We practice. We learn. We collect information that we need to become better at who we are.

If we choose not to learn, we will constantly be given the opportunity to correct ourselves and our choices, hence the bitter-sweet of life patterns.

Sharing our emotions and being willing to learn are productive ways of life. However, we don't always conduct our business in this fashion. Instead of focusing on core issues that we have or reoccurring issues that surface in our life, we may tend to focus on the smaller issues.

Small issues that we focus on daily can be a waste of time. We don't always know or realize that we are complaining so much about these small things either. Some of us complain as though it was second nature. We don't stop to analyze whether what we are saying has actual value to our well-being and those around us.

When we put our complaining into this perspective, we are able to determine the importance of what we are actually communicating to ourselves and the world around us. What we give is what we get.

If we continuously send out distress signals to others we will create panic and ultimately receive that distress in return. Complainers like complainers. Complainers also like listeners. They need an audience to feel like they are getting their point across and validated at the same time.

Complaints and criticism have their place in the world, but it is our goal to determine when it is necessary to complain and when it is not necessary. If frequent complaining affects your overall well-being and constantly gives you a negative picture of the world, then you need to pay attention to what you are saying to yourself and those around you. Your perspective of your environment can determine your attitude towards everything that you encounter. If you have a bad attitude and perceive everything that you encounter as negative then you are constantly sending out this signal of distress.

You will actually draw negative people and behaviors towards yourself simply by the energy you are giving off. Granted, we have situations in life where, yes, negative situations happen to even the most positive people. Having a positive attitude does not prevent us from encountering a negative situation in our lives; a positive attitude does, however, limit the control these situations have over us. Our recovery time from falling down is less. A positive person is able to say, "I will pick myself up and try again."

Complaints come in all shapes and sizes. They can be on a large scale and affect all of us as a world. They can be on a small scale and be complaints that we tell ourselves. What we can do is first realize what we have control over and what we do not have control over. Is our complaint going to initiate a change? Is our complaint going to start changing the way everyone in the world is thinking right now about this subject? Most of the times our complaints are on a smaller scale, but they have a large impact on us and our outlook towards the world around us.

For someone that complains constantly without even realizing it, they might think, "What harm am I essentially causing? After all, I am only complaining to myself." This is actually not true. When you complain out loud, you are essentially filling your own world with negative statements instead of positive. Instead of words of encouragement, you are giving yourself words of stress.

People typically are not just complaining to themselves, they are complaining to friends, family, and even co-workers. Your "disease" becomes their disease. Your affliction becomes their affliction simply by the association alone. Complaints have an impact on others' ideas of illusions.

Thus rumors are derived from people's perspectives and views of particular disputes. They can be based on facts or they can be based on fiction, but no matter what, they can be easily distorted and made proportionate to one's own reality and perspective.

For example, you could complain to five co-workers at the same exact time in the same room about your unhappiness with your employment. Each person will derive their own conclusions and their own outcome. Some of them will even internalize your unhappiness and apply it to their own dissatisfactions. What happens is that a snowball effect occurs and gradually spreads to others that were not even present at the time the initial complaint was issued.

The same can be said for positive feedback about an employer. Let's say, for example, that one person goes in and raves to their co-workers about how well they enjoy their job and the company. Positive comments, of course, don't always spread as rapidly as negative comments. Due to the interest level, negative comments attract other's curiosity more frequently. However, the overall "feeling" of positive feedback versus negative leaves us with a sense of comfort versus a sense of dread.

Not every day can we feel good about what we do or about who we are. That is a simple truth in life. We all have good days and not so good days. We have moments where we doubt our efforts and then we have moments of great satisfaction. Unfortunately, these moments can occur in their own sequence. Although we can't control these moments in our life or guarantee ourselves 100% satisfaction with our goals and efforts, we can show up for what the day has to offer us, whether it is good or challenging.

Our views and perspectives alone can determine the direction we work towards. If we believe something will be bad and we have a bad attitude before we even embark on the endeavor, then we are likely to continue this path until we focus on changing our perspectives.

If we believe that good will come to us and that we are worthy of this goodness, then the outcome of the situation will likely be good. The key to our own success, regardless of the outcome, is simply the attitude we have when we enter the situation.

Take, for example, an even more serious physical situation like medical surgery. If you are determined that you might experience death during the procedure, then this possibly could be your outcome. On the hand, if you are determined that you are going to fight your way through the surgery and put all your efforts into a full recovery, then this will likely be your outcome.

You have the ability to take control of the wheel with your attitude. You may not always be able to control the situation, but you can take control of your perspective of what occurs around you. If you seek positive attributes and benefits from all situations then that is what you will receive. If you seek negative attributes and benefits from your situation, then that is what you will receive in return.

It is not what happens to us in our daily lives that determine how we should feel. It is our attitude about our daily life situations that determines how we perceive ourselves and others.

Our first steps towards acknowledging what is unproductive or productive complaining is to start keeping a journal of what you say on a daily basis. Start writing down your complaints. If you start complaining about cleaning or daily chores then write them down. If you have kids and find yourself becoming stressed and complaining, then write that down. Take notice of what you are verbally saying to yourself and those around you.

Is something bothering you at work and you find yourself spending time on complaining to other co-workers or your family when you come home? Write down your complaints. This will help you determine how often you complain about your daily life and what you complain about.

If you notice you are complaining about one area of your life more than other areas, then you might need to start turning your complaints into actions. If something is taking up your valuable time and causing such a great dissatisfaction to you that you feel you need to spend free time complaining about its presence, then a change needs to be made.

If you notice that you are complaining about yourself, then write down what you are saying to yourself. What negative phrases are slipping out of your mouth? You might be complaining more about yourself than anything else and not even realize it. Taking the time to write down what you are complaining about in a 24-hour period will help you document your current attitude and frame of mind.

Awareness is the first key to our success. There is freedom in knowing who we are and where we are with our daily thoughts and patterns. What takes up our time and energy should be worth our while, not our demise. Focus on where you are placing your energy. Make a commitment to invest time in how you conduct your daily life. Even if you only keep a journal for a week or a month, it would be a beneficial length of time for you to see what area you are dissatisfied with in your life.

Maybe it is work or relationships. Or maybe you will find it is a co-worker or family member that you find yourself focused on. Our primary goal is to revert the focus back onto ourselves, knowing that the time spent is well-deserved and beneficial. When we spend time complaining, we are essentially taking away time from becoming our more perfect self.

Unproductive complaining is just an excuse not to be happy, so make no excuses.

Journal Exercise 1

1. Start writing down your complaints from the time you wake up until the time you go to bed. No matter how big or small the complaints are, write them down. Even if you complain about something not working properly, write it down. Our goal is to see what is coming out of our mouths daily in the form of complaints.

2. Write down all complaints and dissatisfactions with yourself. This is very crucial. If you have a day where you are not happy with the way you look or feel, take note of this. There are times when we think to ourselves, "I don't like this ____ about myself." We might not verbalize our thought, but it is still there so make a note in your journal if any negative thoughts about yourself are present.

3. If there is a daily responsibility that you have to perform and you find yourself complaining about it, then make note of this and write it down. Write down your feelings about your responsibilities if you have something that you dislike.

Chapter 2

taking

OWNERSHIP

We can easily become overwhelmed with our responsibilities. For some of us we have to manage work, family, personal time and time with our companions. Somewhere in between all of the responsibilities that are given to us, we end up adding on even more responsibilities and unfortunately ones that are not necessary for us to own.

When we have children, we are entirely held responsible for their livelihood and the environment we surround them with. They are a priority and a privilege. But what we forget is that not all people that are involved in our lives hold that same priority and responsibility. So therefore, our involvement and control in their lives should be minimal.

Sometimes we can get so involved in other people's business that we allow that to overshadow our own lives and choices. After all, it is an easy task to look into the eyes of another's faults, but a difficult task to look into the eyes of ourselves.

Focusing on others more than ourselves occupies our time falsely, leaving us with an unjust sense of accomplishment. As we are finding solutions or searching for them in someone else's affairs, we are not tending to our own affairs as we should.

When we focus on other people, we are essentially using other people as an excuse not to deal with our issues and ourselves. We seek others' drama only to neglect our own.

Instead, we are masking ourselves and procrastinating our own interventions without even realizing it. It is neither our job nor duty to "straighten" people out. It is, however, our job to be an example for others to follow and take ownership of what we deserve to become.

What ends up happening is we continue to put ourselves off. We continue to make ourselves wait to take on certain challenges and opportunities because we are too busy focusing on others. Other people's goals become our goals instead of us working on developing and creating our own foundations of well-being.

And sure, people do this all the time without even being aware of the situation they put themselves in. Assisting and supporting others is not the issue here; it is enabling and trying to control others that depletes the equation. We are all placed in this world to better our situations and conditions. As long as we agree to allow others to live freely, we create room for growth and new opportunities.

We do not have to limit people by what we think they can accomplish. As when we attempt to control people, that is exactly what we are doing: placing limitations on them where certain limitations should not exist. We have to leave some creativity up to the universe to do as it intended with whom it is intended.

When we release ourselves from this control, we open up more time for ourselves to focus on achieving our own potential. We take hold of what we have to work with and go forward.

So essentially we are removing the release and the hold that we have on people, places, and things that we do not own or have control over. We are releasing these things to become what they were intended to be, not what we thought they should become. We are allowing the path of the world to take over in areas where it should.

This only allows us to center our focus on who we do have control over, ourselves. This is a journey in itself that will allow us more time and less complaining, more focus and less disagreements.

Try to imagine yourself standing in a crowd of people. The people or situations, whatever applies to your life, are in front of you. It is difficult to shine your light outwards if you are trying to hide within the crowd. So give yourself space to become that in which you were intended to be.

What we are doing here is removing unnecessary responsibilities from our lives. We are opening our time and energy up for ourselves. This is not a selfish choice; it is a selfish obligation, meaning that we are obligated to invest time in ourselves if we want to grow.

The moment we acknowledge our involvement in our own lives is the moment we admit to ourselves that we want to change. We want to become better people. We want to use our time here more efficiently and effectively.

This is not to say that time spent on others is wasteful, because that is not the case at all. It is time that we spend trying to "fix" others' behaviors and not our own that becomes time-consuming.

We have to come to the realization that people around us are going to do what they want to do regardless of what we say to them. It is ultimately their own will that is the deciding factor, not ours. Sure we can have an impact on people; our living example alone can have such power, but are we the decision maker for all? No. Nor is it our job to be.

There is a lot of unnecessary frustration that can stem from trying to control another person's actions. We have to come to the point in our lives when we stop and realize what we are doing. What is causing us to complain? What is causing an inner sense of frustration? When we take that time to evaluate our actions with others, we are essentially pinpointing our time busters.

If we feel that other people are the cause of our frustration then it is time to look for a healthy solution to resolve our turmoil. Search out what is blocking you and then make an effort to find a resolution. Perhaps it means no longer participating. You may need to physically stop reacting and remove yourself from the person you are trying to control so that you can assess your involvement. Everyone has that option but sometimes they do not realize they do. Know that it is okay to stand up and walk away when your interaction with this person or situation is doing more harm than good.

The perfect example is for people involved with unhealthy relationships where emotional and physical abuses are present. We can all feel some sort of compassion and even empathy towards the person that is involved; however, if we put it in perspective, and look outside the situation instead of in, we can see another side.

The person enduring the abuse has a choice. No matter how you look at the situation, no matter how complicated the situation may be, the fact in the matter is that both people involved have a choice. And until one of them starts to alter their choices and decisions, the unhealthy patterns will continue.

Imagine that you are in a wading pool and you are swimming around; you start to panic and start drowning. Well the reality is, all you need to do is stand up. The same theory can be applied to your life. Stand up. You have that right. You have that power to walk away from people, places, or things that do not benefit your health.

Anything unhealthy to us depletes our energy. It robs us of the valuable energy that we need to succeed in life. Having unhealthy relationships or involvements with others is unnatural. In modern times, we may look at this or accept that this should be our normality, but it doesn't have to be. We have the choice to accept our life on other terms. We were meant to be happy. We were intended to be challenged, not depleted.

Think of it this way: does it not seem like the happiest moments in our lives went the quickest? That is because joy, happiness, and love add to our energy, not take away, so the amount of time spent can be less. When we get stuck in unhealthy conditions that we do have control over, time begins to lag. We begin to feel exhausted all the time. Our energy levels become depleted and we may seek even more unhealthy solutions to compensate.

Instead of stepping back from our problems and making a valid assessment, people can contribute to their own demise, and spin even further away from their own awareness. People may find remedy in drugs, alcohol, smoking, or even overeating, all of which does not solve the problem; it only temporarily removes you from the turmoil. However this removal is an illusion.

The reality is that when we are searching for outside remedies, we are merely procrastinating and distancing ourselves from a solution. If the stove is hot, don't touch it. It is that easy. If you are in a situation that does not feel good to you and/or does not feel right, get up and walk away.

If you can accept the reality of who you have control over, you can accept the freedom that will be offered to you from release of burdens not your own.

Children and the elderly are an exception to this rule, but grown responsible adults have the right to take care of themselves. They have the right to make decisions just as we do.

Start by making an active assessment of your responsibilities. Make two columns. On the left-hand side write at the top for a heading, "Things I "think" I am responsible for". Then in the right-hand column, write "Things I am responsible for".

In the first column place all the things you "think" you are responsible for. It can be jobs. It can be people, places, or things. Whatever you feel that you are responsible for, write it down.

The next column is your reality-revealing column. Take time to evaluate everything that you wrote in the left column and assess if this is a necessary responsibility or an unnecessary responsibility.

When you are all done look at the outcome, does one side outweigh the other? Does the column on the left outweigh the column on the right? Or does the assessment come out evenly? If the left side weighs heavier, then you need to perhaps work on eliminating responsibilities that are not your own. By doing so you will free up time, space, and energy and be able to eliminate complaining in the long run.

Journal Exercise 2

1. Start by making an active assessment of your responsibilities. Make two columns. On the left-hand side write at the top for a heading, "Things I "think" I am responsible for". Then in the right-hand column, write "Things I am responsible for".

2. In the first column place all the things you "think" you are responsible for. It can be jobs. It can be people, places, or things. Whatever you feel that you are responsible for, write it down.

3. The next column is your reality-revealing column. Take time to evaluate everything that you wrote in the left column and assess if this is a necessary responsibility or an unnecessary responsibility.

4. When you are all done look at the outcome. Does one side outweigh the other? Does the column on the left outweigh the column on the right? Or does the assessment come out evenly? If the left side weighs heavier, then you need to perhaps work on eliminating

responsibilities that are not your own. By doing so you will free up time, space, and energy and be able to eliminate complaining in the long run.

5. Start a new page after you have performed this exercise and at the top of your page write down in big letters the word ACTION. Write down what action you plan on taking to eliminating unnecessary responsibilities. What changes do you need to make? What goals do you want to set that could help you operate more efficiently as a person? Think about both your short and long term goals and then write them down. Allow yourself at least six months for any major life changes. Sometimes a change of attitude or perspective can occur within this time frame and we find that action within ourselves was what was needed, not an action depending on someone else.

Chapter 3

Verbal Complaints

How often do you find yourself complaining out loud to others or perhaps to yourself? What about even saying complaints under your breath while you think nobody hears you? You may think your complaints fall on deaf ears, but they do not. There is someone that hears you: the universe and your inner self.

The verbal cues that you provide yourself with are generally reflected in your attitude and perspective of the world around you. Where the mind goes, the body will follow. We can literally make ourselves sick. Our words and our attitude have such a crucial impact on our bodies. An example would be a child who "fakes" that they are sick so they do not have to go to school. They go around acting sick around their parents. They act out their ailments. They portray themselves as too ill to do anything. The parent agrees after assessing their condition and before the child knows it, their sickness becomes a reality.

The same scenario occurs even as we age, but the person we portray our complaints to might be our spouse instead of our parents, or worse yet, ourselves. Verbalization is a very strongly engaged form of self-talk. When we start verbally complaining about our lives, or our daily livelihood, we create a breeding ground for negativity. This breeding ground attracts more than what we may initially desire.

For example, everyone ages differently. Some people choose to grow old gracefully. They may even term themselves as 75 years young versus 75 years old. They wake up and greet their day with a smile and a positive outlook. They take the experiences that they have acquired and continue to look forward to a tomorrow.

Then there are people that have a negative attitude about aging and they only reinforce their thoughts onto themselves by referencing how old they are, and how their age impedes their functions. They consume themselves with negative thoughts and self talk so that soon their health reflects their minds. Where the mind travels, the body will follow.

When you are constantly complaining, people will hear you. They will see the facial expressions. They will feel your frustrations. Positive energy providers will naturally overlook this initially. Positive people want to save the world. They want to make it better. They want people to feel better and they will go great lengths to stride towards universal improvements. However, if the complaints persist around you, eventually even those with positive outlooks will not enjoy your presence.

The old saying that "misery loves company" is certainly true here. Eventually after enough complaining, the only people that will want to hang around you are complainers themselves. They will be the only ones that desire to be around your negativity, primarily because they release negativity themselves.

Just as there are positive self-talking mantras, there are also negative binding mantras. Verbal complaining only reiterates our anger. It is the fuel of the fire. What happens is this repetitive complaining out loud eventually affects our view of our environment, our immediate surroundings, our view of others and our view of ourselves.

Instead of assuring ourselves that we can do something, we are assuring ourselves that we cannot do something. Instead of finding a solution, we are creating a problem. In this regard, our complaints are not initiating a positive action; instead, they are initiating depression, disappointment, and lack of motivation.

No matter how small the complaint, when spoken out loud the complaint takes on a whole new construction. Our verbal cue is voicing to the universe that there is not a solution, that there is not a positive outlook to the matter at hand. We are reiterating to ourselves that we are stuck and we don't know how to 'get out' or find resolution. We end up stifling our own progress in our lives as we create an obstacle in our mind that we end up having issues diverting.

Instead of saying, "I CAN DO THIS" a complainer might say, "I CAN'T DO THIS." A complainer might say "I CAN'T TAKE THIS ANYMORE" instead of "I WILL TRY MY BEST." These verbal cues repeated over and over will yield different results. We can choose to create a negative space or a positive space for ourselves. We can consider this mental housekeeping a crucial part of our well-being. If we give ourselves something to look forward to in our lives, we give ourselves a reason to live and a reason to be happy.

Remember there will always be valid complaints in our lives, but our goal is to eliminate the complaints that are not valid and are more so thieves of time, versus catalysts for change.

We need to start realizing how important what we say and what we do are. We need to stop thinking that we are only affecting ourselves or not even affecting anything at all. Once we start viewing ourselves in a different light, we may finally understand how important what we say and do on a daily basis reflects on those around us, including our universe as a whole. Our complaints and negativity can pollute more than just the immediate people around us. Our complaints can travel further then we think.

Over-complaining and disregarding ourselves as having value just breaks down our self-esteem, leaving us with even more complaints waiting to snowball over top of even more complaints.

Start validating yourself. If you are not a positive person then work towards changing that aspect of yourself. If there is something you can't do and you want to do, then fake it until you make it. Be your own actor and play the part you want to be. Even if you don't feel in your heart you can, play the game with yourself by acting the role. Use the laws of gravity to your benefit, not to your own destruction. We mentioned before that where the mind travels, the body would follow. This is the same concept except we are choosing to use our mind to empower the positive in our lives instead of the negative.

Our own verbal complaints are crucial to our well-being as they interpret our outcome. If we anticipate success, we will have success. If we anticipate failure, then that is what we will achieve because that is our outlook. If you are climbing up a mountain, you don't want to look down, as your body will likely follow. You want to look up. You want to look towards the direction you are intending to head and for us that means progressing forward.

Everyone has highs and lows that we encounter in life. How we view these moments can determine how we are able to cope during certain circumstances. Striving for a positive outlook during the lows in our lives can be crucial to our perseverance and our ability to overcome obstacles.

Our own verbal cues are crucial; however, those around us providing their verbal opinions of our lives can be crucial as well. We are trained individuals. We are raised to think a certain trait or behavior is wrong and other behaviors are good. We were scolded for doing wrong and rewarded for good based on cues from our parental units. We then carry these cues on to our lives in adulthood.

In a perfect world we can assume that all parents are perfect and gave us a perfect foundation to build our life upon, but this is not always the case. And as we bare the fruits of adulthood we then find out the rules in the home we were raised in do not always apply to rules of the world. We then find out there are other rights and other wrongs and it is our responsibility to determine which we prefer to adhere to.

With our freedom of choice we will encounter responsibility. But we will always have the foundation set by our parents or family that will remain in the background. Again, this is wonderful if your upbringing was of great satisfaction. But for those of you who had negative verbal cues that were introduced to you as a child, then you can replay these negative "tapes" over and over even in your adult life.

If you had a great deal of criticism growing up, then you are likely going to constantly be overly critical with yourself. This just goes to show us the longevity induced by not only our own verbalizations, but also someone else's verbalizations. Not only are we what we think we are, but we can also be influenced by what others think of us as well.

We want to please the teacher. We want to be a good student. We want to feel as though we have the approval of our parents or guardians. So we learn these cues, but they are not always rewarded. Unfortunately, sometimes our goodness and our capabilities can verbally be disregarded by our teachers, our parents. This is a crucial correction that we have to make as we walk forward to adulthood, as we need to retrain ourselves to think higher of ourselves versus lower.

There isn't always going to be someone there that pats you on the back and tells you that you are a worthy person. There isn't always going to be someone there that says you got an "A" on that or you deserve a promotion. At some point in our lives we need to not look towards others for approving and validating our good behaviors. Instead we need to look towards ourselves and realize that, yes, we are capable of being good and capable of doing good for others and ourselves.

Verbal complaints and criticisms from others don't have a shelf life. They can be carried with us for as long as we feel they have value to us and for as long as we allow them to affect us. It could be one small thing that someone said to us: for example, "you will never amount to anything," and we will either spend our lifetime proving him or her wrong or proving them right.

Taking time out to identify some of the derivatives of our insecurities is crucial for changing our outlook. There is a root to our behaviors. There is a reason why we have moments of doubt; either we have verbally discouraged ourselves or others have verbally discouraged us.

A good example is when someone has an idea they want to set out to accomplish and someone in their immediate circle says, "You can't do that; that's not going to work." This simple phrase alone has a lot of verbal power, whether this person realizes this or not. There is a tremendous weight that this phrase provides to the person trying to communicate their idea. Any opposition faced during the preliminary development of a goal or idea can impact the person initiating the concept. They will either feel confident or they might feel foolish.

Our success depends on our confidence and ability to set out and achieve that which we believe in. If we have a foundation that allows us the freedom to experiment and feel confident with the thoughts that we develop then we are very apt to set forth our ideas. However, if our foundation is weakened and we are insecure with our ideas, we are less likely to feel confident about setting out to achieve them. It all depends on the foundation that they have upon the creation of the concept. Do they feel confident that no matter what someone says to impede their progress that they will continue to go seek success? Or do they feel unsure and have a lack of confidence to overcome slight differences of opinion?

This verbal complaint creates doubt. Whereas, if someone says, "I think that's a great idea," instantly validation is given to the idea owner.

So ultimately our goal is to identify verbal cues that we have either given ourselves or that others have provided us with, sort them out to whether they are a help or a hindrance, and then replace negative verbal cues with positive ones. Sometimes we have to rewrite the book, we have to rebuild the foundation we started out with. We can rebuild anytime we choose to; we just have to be willing to look at ourselves and those around us in a very realistic view. We need to see our errors and then set forth to correct them and make changes based on the beliefs we have now.

Listen to yourself. Do you find yourself saying, "I can't" instead of "I can"? Look and see where this is coming from. Ask yourself the right questions. Ask yourself why you feel that way. Take time to trace the origin of your own doubts. It was the great philosopher Socrates that said, "The *unanalyzed life is not worth living.*"

Verbal cues from others can have a life of their own that live on even after their owners have passed or are no longer present in our lives. Our memories are like tape recorders that secure each word whether bitter or sweet and save them for a later time. We recall these verbal tapes at times when a situation reoccurs in our lives.

Our low points in life can trigger prior situations where either we were told we couldn't achieve something or we thought this of ourselves. Certain points may trigger us where our self-esteem was damaged. We might recall a situation where we did not feel that we were in control of the outcome and we felt powerless. We might recall what someone has said to us or recall someone's doubts in our abilities. All of these life situations come into a complete circle, constantly providing us with the opportunity to correct our past behaviors.

One of the finer beautiful gifts of our lives here on earth is that the universe allows us to correct our behaviors by recycling situations that we failed to achieve the first time around. Did you ever notice that our relationship with partners continues a pattern until we recognize the pattern and are willing to change it? For example, we may always start relationships with people that are on a rebound out of another serious relationship and the outcome is always the same. The person appreciates our friendship, but is not ready to commit to another serious situation.

When we look at the facts first and separate our emotional commitment to something or someone, we can analyze the truth of the situation and then prevent ourselves from being involved in situations that might prove to be heartbreaking in the end. We can actually foresee the situation because it is one we have repeated many times and had the same results. If we stop to think of the end results and we actually consider what the outcome is, we can step back from the situation, view the facts, and then decide if we want to proceed with involving ourselves further.

Life is a strategic game; there are certain methods that we need to mentally attain to conquer and achieve new levels and stages of enlightenment. If we don't learn now, we will not continue to evolve. We will continue to be complacent and stagnant. We will continue to complain and therefore continue our own patterns of self-discouragement.

We need to become aware that there is a bigger picture than what we realize. We were intended to be of great mind and body. However, in life there will always be challenges that will try to destroy this greatness. It is up to us to recognize these occurrences and continue to move forward with strength.

We have the ability to choose the verbal cues we wish to overwrite and which ones we wish to keep. We can take ownership of what we want to listen to and what we want to disregard. We can take what we want and leave the rest. We can replace the negative with positive. We can use what we have learned and rise above the situation.

Our goal is to improve our own quality of life. Our situation and our environment can remain the same, but it is our opinions and our outlook that can change and actually determine the path that lies ahead. This is a crucial part of creating a well-balanced life and an environment that is worthy of growth and not of strife.

It isn't what material belongings we have or surround ourselves with. True happiness comes when we can stand alone with nothing and still have a smile on our face and a positive attitude in our heart. This is the feeling that provides longevity and greatness. This is the feeling that provides fulfillment and nourishment to the soul.

It is not the car in the driveway, it is the not the big house, or the wallet filled with money. It is the sincere part of one's self that gives us the ability to say I am what I am. I have what I need. I am content with the person I am and I am content with the person I intend to be.

You can watch people all the time, observe their behaviors. You can compare the rich and you can compare the poor. Not everyone that is poor is miserable and not everyone that is rich is sincerely happy. You will find complainers among them both.

What it all comes down to is the type of person you are and hold true to be. If you had nothing in your hands and nothing around you, would you still be kind to others? Would you still be kind to yourself? If you had nothing would you still find a way to be happy with what you have? Would you still have a positive outlook on your life?

Granted, our environments and living conditions can always have a factor on our attitudes, but our challenge in life is when we are presented with such conditions, what type of attitude we will choose to maintain.

There are two types of people we can term ourselves to be; either we are considered the complainer or the optimist. The complainer will repeat the difficulty over and over in their minds and even verbalize their situation and perhaps not take a course of action. Whereas the optimist will look for a resolution and during this time of difficulty perhaps keep to themselves until the issue is sorted.

The optimist might speak with a close confidant or if one is not around they may seek some other means of relieving frustrations. Whereas, the complainer might choose to use negative outlets of release, such as inflicting harm on themselves as a way of self-punishment. They might opt to indulge in a negative behavior. They might choose to take their frustrations out on other people around them. They might use their frustrations as an excuse to be inactive and unmotivated.

Our responses to the situations that we encounter are the key to our balance and well-being. Our responses represent how we feel about ourselves and the world around us. Are we confident? Or are we unsure? Our attitudes reflect our nature in general,; *where the mind travels, the body will follow.*

Everyone has not so good days or days where they are not on top of the world. Whether you are considered an optimist or a complainer, you will encounter these life fluctuations. For every low there is a high, and for every high there is a low.

Our verbal cues and responses to these situations determine the longevity of our discomfort and the longevity of our joy. Did you ever see someone having something positive occur to them and they are so stuck in being negative that they can't even enjoy themselves or the moment? No matter what, they are determined to find fault even amongst joy?

When we constantly seek or hear ourselves complaining this becomes a part of our lives. The criticism then carries over to even moments when no criticism should be made. Instead of believing that everything is "okay" the complainer will seek for something to not be "okay" even in the most perfect situations. They will choose to find imperfections.

Our verbal cues are affected by our attitude and our ability to function in any given life situation. We can determine how well we are able to recover in a situation based on our attitude. Are we going to look up or are we going to look down?

The only way to identify the verbal cues in your life is first to pay attention to them. What are you constantly hearing either from yourself or from other people? What tapes are playing in your mind? If for some reason you think you cannot succeed in life, why? Who or what made you think differently?

Stop to realize what you are up against. Are you up against yourself or are you up against others? Are both others and you affecting your self-image? Nothing is worse than allowing yourself to get in your own way. Self-defeat is often the largest hurdle that one can try to overcome as we are always with ourselves. We can't run from our own negativity; all we can do is learn to change our outlook and change our behaviors.

If you have anything in your life that is preventing you from seeing your own patterns then it is time to identify those obstacles and remove anything that is no longer of benefit to you. If you have surrounded yourself with negative people then the only way you are going to clear the path and shed a little light on your own self-value is to start spending less of your time with negative people and more of your time with positive people.

If you want a better outlook in life sometimes you have to make major life changes. You may have to separate from negative situations or people. Sometimes the person can just be yourself and the way you were always trained to view the world around you.

Now is the time to challenge yourself and identify your downfalls and heighten your greatness. Document and write down in a journal what repetitive phrases you hear on a daily basis. If someone says something to you, or if you find yourself complaining about something, write it down. Take your notebook with you and when you hear a complaint write it down. Or just write them all down at the end of the day.

Sometimes we do not realize the frequency of our negative verbal cues until they are written down before us. Look and see if your page is full or is it empty? Once you have completed a daily journal of your complaints then you can start to recognize the patterns that might be occurring daily. You will be able to notice when you feel your worst, or might even begin to recognize slight triggers in your own attitude after a verbal cue is given.

After you have written your quick list of verbal cues, then follow up and make notes on your thoughts or emotions. Did you find that these verbal cues were self-defeating? Did they make you feel better or worse? How did these affect your attitude?

Our primary goal is to achieve happiness in all areas of our lives. If something is off balance, if something is out of place, then our happiness is compromised. And if we don't actually stop to realize how this is occurring we can't always defend ourselves against it.

So taking this time to analyze where or why we are complaining or feeling dissatisfaction in our lives can be crucial to our overall well-being. Examples of imbalances can be overeating or indulgence in alcohol or drug abuse. For some people smoking or adultery can come in to play. Any time we harm others, or ourselves it is a deep inner reflection on our dissatisfaction with ourselves.

Some people are able to identify their behaviors and correct them and some people choose never to make the correction. Instead, they continue to carry out the behaviors they know best and instead of filling in the gaps of their lives, the gaps' distance increase with age and they continue to deepen them.

We can grow towards our true selves or grow away from our true selves. It all depends on what we choose to clutter our inner being with. We have positive aspirations and we have negativity that we have to battle with and often redirect.

Journal Exercise 3

1. In our prior exercises, we focused on the complaints that we ourselves say daily. Now we are going to focus on what we hear from others around us either about us or about others to determine how much negativity we are encountering daily. Document and write down in a journal what repetitive phrases you hear on a daily basis. If someone says something to you, or if you find yourself complaining about something, write it down. Take your notebook with you and when you hear a complaint write it down. Or just write them down at the end of the day.

2. When you are finished with the first exercise, look and see if your page is full or is it empty? Once you have completed a daily journal of complaints then you can start to recognize the patterns that might be occurring daily. You will be able to notice when you feel your worst, or might even begin to recognize slight triggers in your own attitude after a verbal cue is given.

3. After you have written your quick list of verbal cues, then follow up and make notes on your thoughts or

emotions. Did you find that these verbal cues were self-defeating? Did they make you feel better or worse? How did these affect your attitude?

4. Taking this time to analyze where or why we are complaining or feeling dissatisfaction in our lives can be crucial to our overall well-being. Examples of imbalances can be overeating or indulgence in alcohol or drug abuse. For some people smoking or adultery can come in to play. Any time we harm ourselves or harm others, it is a deep inner reflection on our dissatisfaction with ourselves. Write down any imbalances you feel that you have currently and then make notes on what you can do to change them now that you are recognizing them.

Chapter 4

redirecting

Energy

We don't live in a perfect world and as soon as we are willing to accept that fact alone we will be able to better understand the way in which life progresses. We have two ways of viewing the changes we encounter. We can view them as positive or we can view them as negative.

Change is life's way of promoting our career as human beings. We are constantly presented with challenges and situations that will permit us to make positive or negative choices. If we encounter an issue in our lives and make the wrong decision, we will later on in life be presented with a situation very similar. Our situations can become recycled, where the situation is the same and only the characters change. These reoccurring life presentations do not occur by accident. This is the universe's way of allowing you an opportunity to practice making the right choice.

An example is someone in an unhealthy relationship that says to their confidant, "I don't know why this keeps happening to me. I don't know why I always find these types of partners." Well, the truth is, we are constantly presented with situations in life that can either better or worsen us. If you keep encountering the negative then perhaps it is because you keep choosing the negative. You will continue to choose the negative until you finally redirect the energy to positive and change your pattern of choice.

The concept alone appears to be so simple and it is, but when you have a clouded mind, you don't always see the pattern. You see part of the picture instead of looking at the whole.

Identifying patterns and recognizing reoccurring situations will help us look at our choices and learn how to better them. Start analyzing your life and the people that encompass your surroundings. Who are you surrounding yourself with? Are you surrounding yourself with people that believe in you? Or are you surrounding yourself with people you feel don't believe in you and are not supportive?

Are you a part of the drama or are you the creator of drama? We refer to drama in the sense where a life situation is taken beyond the bounds of proportion and is exploded into a level of intensity that draws others towards you. Do you need help or are you the helper? Do you deal with your own life drama or are you too busy trying to help others deal with their drama?

Some people jump from one issue to the next. Instead of coming to a balance they are constantly seeking situations that place them over the edge. They will either re-enact this in their own lives or become a parasite onto others' life situations when they cannot find their own.

Life dramas are essentially excuses to not focus on our aspirations in life. Granted, we have real life situations that we can be a part of, but there are also unnecessary dramas that we either invite or attract that's only purpose is to distract us from moving forward to our purpose.

To help us realign our inner balance we need to assess where we are currently. We will do this by performing a series of journal entries that will help us evaluate where we are and where we intend on being. The steps will be repeated at the end of the chapter in a concise format to make it less overwhelming when you begin the journal entry section. So read this section first for absorption and then read the journal entry section for clarity.

There are several questions we can ask ourselves to help us determine the quality of life we have right now and the quality of life we wish to pursue:

1. Do you constantly find drama in your life or do you surround yourself with people that have dramatized issues? This is an important question to ask yourself as your energy can easily be devoted to someone else's dramas if you don't pay attention, or become aware of this.

There is nothing wrong with us wanting to help other people; however, it is when we take on a responsibility that is not our own that we become a hindrance more than a help. We can term ourselves as an *enabler*, a person that helps others remain sick. Instead of putting out the fire, we feed it. Some wars in life are intended to be battled by their owners. We can be an example. We can show others what they too can accomplish, but we can't do it for them.

It is just like a child; you can hold their hand, but you can't walk for them. They have to have the desire to want to accomplish the goal.

If you are the drama in your life then whether you realize it or not, you find some sort of pleasure directing attention to your life in a negative way versus positive. We term this as negative because of the amount of energy that is extracted from others you involve during your dramas. Your helpers or your confidants will become emotionally drained just trying to seek a resolution for your inability or lack of making positive life choices.

Take time to assess which role you might play in people's lives or your own. Perhaps neither category identifies you, or perhaps at one time it did. Write down what you can relate to or what you surround yourself with now if this is the case.

2. Do you feel balanced or at peace with your life? If not, what areas do you feel that you need to improve on? Disruptions in our lives are there for a reason. They allow us to feel uncomfortable enough in one situation that we seek something new. We seek a change to better our situation or make us feel different than the way we feel now. This can mean discomfort in your physical location, or it can also represent our inner well being, where we feel uncomfortable with the people we are around or our life ambitions, so we seek new and more meaningful ways of presenting ourselves.

3. What life situations do you find keep reoccurring? Is there any pattern? Writing this area of your life down will help you identify the pattern and then see what you can do to change it. If you keep encountering partners that are emotionally draining to you then perhaps that is because you keep choosing people that are at a constant stage of fluctuation in their life. You might actually be seeking people that are unstable, instead of seeking people that are stable. So ask yourself why this is the case. If you removed this obstacle, if you removed the barrier, and actually made a choice for stability, would you not know how to be with someone? Are you so accustomed to a particular reoccurring role that you only feel needed in the relationship if the partner is unstable?

Or another situation could be with your career, where you are constantly picking positions that are not challenging or a part of your overall aspirations, which can become draining and almost self-defeating.

4. What changes do you want to make about yourself or the type of people you surround yourself with? Are you healthy? Do you exercise your mind, body, and spirit? Are you surrounding yourself with like-minded people? Or are you surrounding yourself with people that are constantly challenging your beliefs?

Our primary goal in life is to further our aspirations and always find meaning. If we always feel as though we are hitting a brick wall with people or situations then we are being stifled and confined where our energy can become stale.

When we begin to feel stale what happens is that energy might be turned inward and against ourselves, instead of for ourselves. That's where our over-indulgences come in to play. We might use them to comfort our emotions and numb our awareness. The indulgence provides us with movement, therefore leaving a false sense of satisfaction to the mind. This false sense of satisfaction is temporary. We enjoy the moment, but not the consequence.

An example of this would be someone that we'll say works all day, comes home, and then out of boredom, gorges themselves with food at night. Instead of taking that energy and converting it into something useful, they turn it inward and make the normal life necessity of "food" an imbalance.

Our energy is such a powerful source that when not diverted or directed properly it can be used against us. So think of ways that you might use, or have used your energy against yourself in your life. Are you empowering yourself with your energy or are you depleting yourself of energy by using it towards irrelevant tasks? This could mean consuming yourself with others issues that are not your responsibility. This could mean using your time towards addictions instead of successes.

Our goal with this exercise is energy conservation. We want to make sure that we are not wasting our energy on people, places, or things that we ultimately have no control over anyway. We want to refocus ourselves to the one thing we do have control over and that is ourselves.

5. What negative influences are around me now? Remember negativity breeds negativity. So it is crucial that we take time to identify what might be draining us emotionally or physically.

The key in identifying negative people or situations is awareness. We have to have awareness so that we can see the negative versus the positive. This is where our self-judgment comes into place. When we identify negative obstructions in our lives: people, places, obsessions, and addictions, we are clearing a path for growth. This is a magical moment in our lives. When we remove our obstacles, when we remove the things in life that bind us, we are telling the universe that we are willing to be aware and we are willing to be present in this world. We are willing to see as we were intended.

When we have obstructions present around us or self-inflicted then we are unable to see clearly. An example of an obstruction is an unhealthy relationship. We use relationships as an example as it is something all of us involve ourselves in at one point or another in our lives and can relate to on different levels. As human beings we are constantly interacting with one another. Let's say we have two alcoholics that come together to have a relationship with one another. How often do we hear that a relationship with an alcoholic is healthy? Or how often do we hear someone say, "I have a partner who is an alcoholic and our relationship is just great"?

Granted, some people in unhealthy situations are disillusioned so that to them, their relationship is essentially perfect and they have something there, but often the relationship is based on the priority, which is drinking. Anything in our lives done out of gluttony can put us off balance and cause us to make irrational decisions or behave in a way that is abnormal to our balanced selves.

So evaluate the people you have present in your life. What people, places or things around you appear to drain your energy? What exhausts you? What leaves you feeling emotionally drained? You may think you do not have something negative in your life until you actually stop and write it down. If you don't have any situation currently that you feel drains your energy, perhaps write about past people, places, or things so that you have a point of reference.

6. What positive influences are around me? There are great moments in our lives when we just feel energized by someone's presence around us. We feel good talking to certain people. We feel energized and hopeful. Write down moments that are going on currently or moments that you can remember where you felt motivated after being around someone.

Maybe it was a whole group of people. Maybe it was a certain location. Just take note on when you felt a real positive charge from people, places, or things.

When we feel positive vibes from people we enjoy being around them and feeling their presence. The only time we do not appreciate their presence is when we are in a negative state of affairs. If we are participating in a lifestyle that is negative then our positive counterparts may not want to be around us very often simply because either it is draining to them or they do not have much in common with someone leading a life with negativity present.

7. Do I spend more time around positive or negative people? Now that we have taken the time to evaluate what negative and positive forces are present in our lives we can assess which of the two we have more of. If you have more positive people present in your life then you likely have a great support system in place for your current goals and ambitions. If you see that you are spending more time with negative people versus positive than you are likely losing energy instead of gaining.

8. What is your plan of action? If you are spending more time with negative people or situations then what form of action are you going to take to change this? Do you want to change this? What effect has having certain negativity in your life had on you?

Often, change is a very difficult action to initiate, especially for those who do not always appreciate the benefits that change brings. Bad habits are hard to break. If constantly feeling depleted and finding yourself surrounded by negative-minded people is something that you are accustomed to, then you might find the pattern difficult to break away from.

The best thing to try is to break away in spurts. Take a week or two to just stay away from any outside drama or negativity that you would normally participate in and compare how you feel with how you did feel. Your challenge is to replace the negative with positive so that you are not left feeling alone or unfulfilled. Use your time to be creative or do something that you enjoy.

If you honestly don't know what you enjoy doing then use this time that you have taken away from negative people to find out more about yourself. Use this time to try new things or to challenge yourself personally. You might actually uncover a different side of yourself that you never saw or experienced before.

Consider this a personal vacation for you. Yes, in the real world many of us will have to work while doing this. And if this is the case, at least try to be slightly strict with yourself and not work overtime for a week. So when you do put your time in you can come home and have your personal vacation away.

9. What areas of my life are neglected? This could be family or true friends. This could be yourself and perhaps certain areas of upkeep. We always hear of people that "let themselves go," meaning they forgot to take care of themselves because they were so involved with others or their own downfall.

When you do take your personal vacation, take time to perform some outside appearance maintenance on yourself. Maybe you need some new clothes. Maybe you need a haircut or a change. Take care of yourself and conscientiously enjoy doing it.

Maybe the opposite is true and you have only been thinking about yourself and neglecting to think about your loved ones. Maybe someone has shown you loyalty and dedication and you have not reciprocated his or her affections and need to. True friends and family will love us unconditionally so it is important to make sure we respond to their needs in addition to our own. If we are going through a difficult time in our lives then let them know that. Don't just avoid people that care about you because you are having a hard time in your life. Sometimes that is exactly what we need to be around: people that care for our well-being and have our best interest at heart.

10. Once we figure out the people, places, and things that we have neglected in our lives, it is our duty to figure out what course of action that we will

take on to induce a change. What are we going to do to correct the neglect? What course of action do we plan on making to reverse our own self-neglect or our neglect on others?

In our society, we are misguided that money can substitute time, but it does not. No money can replace the value and importance that someone's time can have. It is crucial that we make note of what our priorities in life are. Do we place finances and material items above people? Are we constantly spending more time at work than we do with the ones we love? What can we do to change this? What sacrifices are we willing to make to better our lives? Are we willing to do whatever it takes? How bad do we want to be happy?

Journal Exercise 4

1. Do you constantly find drama in your life or do you surround yourself with people that have dramatized issues?

2. Do you feel balanced or at peace with your life? If not, what areas do you feel that you need to improve on?

3. What life situations do you find keep reoccurring? Is there any pattern?

4. What changes do you want to make about yourself or the type of people you surround yourself with? Are you healthy? Do you exercise your mind, body, and spirit? Are you surrounding yourself with like-minded people? Or are you surrounding yourself with people that are constantly challenging your beliefs?

5. What negative influences are around me now?

6. What positive influences are around me?

7. Do I spend more time around positive or negative people?

8. What is your plan of action? If you are spending more time with negative people or situations then what form of action are you going to take to change this? Do you want to change this? What effect has having certain negativity in your life had on you?

9. What areas of my life are neglected?

10. Once we figure out the people, places, and things that we have neglected in our lives it is our duty to figure out what course of action that we will take on to induce a change. What are we going to do to correct the neglect? What course of action do we plan on making to reverse our own self-neglect or our neglect on others?

Chapter 5

the right to be
HAPPY

We can easily become overwhelmed with our responsibilities. There are a great number of people in the world that consider themselves to be miserable and instead of going and evaluating personally the cause, they are seeking medication to be the band-aid. In reality it is only a temporary solution to a more permanent problem. *According to Charles Barber, author of Comfortably Numb: How Psychiatry Is Medicating a Nation, "In 2006, 227 million antidepressant prescriptions were dispensed to Americans–more than any other class of medication–and up by 30 million prescriptions since 2002."*[3]

---

[3] Antidepressant Overload in 'Comfortably Numb'
http://www.npr.org/templates/story/story.php?storyId=89882885

We are entitled to our own greatness. We are entitled to be happy, but for some reason fear sets foot in our lives and we forget our purpose. We were not intended to have a life of pain or a life of sorrow, nor were we intended to spend our time complaining about it. Over half of life's stress or difficulty is not caused by others or situations; it is caused by ourselves responding negatively to the occurrences around us.

We can make ourselves have a positive attitude or a negative attitude. We can start our day however we choose to. If we have a positive attitude then no matter what we encounter, we will accept it as is and take the moment as it stands, not as we have planned it to be. If we start our day with a negative attitude then even the minutest change in the course of our day will disrupt us personally.

What is the difference between positive people and negative people? The difference is that one is willing to "let go" of the reigns and take whatever the universe has to offer them and the other is holding tight to their control. We can compare this to walking or trying to bike ride against the wind. If we go against the wind we have a hard time moving forward, if we go with the wind we are almost carried effortlessly to our destination.

Let's not fool ourselves; positive people with positive attitudes can have some very destructive days, but the difference is their reaction to the destruction. Do they start making excuses to perform bad acts on themselves? Or do they try to do something positive for themselves to occupy their minds as a coping mechanism? Do they start being rude to other people and taking it out on them? Or do they go and talk to a friend or family member about their day and what they feel they should do.

Our role and the role we allow other people to play in our lives are very important. We control the amount of negative people and the amount of positive people that we subject ourselves too. Often times we pick people that match ourselves. So if we are in a negative mind frame then we might start hanging around other like-minded people. Then what happens is we start to feed that negativity back and forth. The same is certainly true for positive people choosing to unite with other positive people.

Did you ever walk into a room where there was an argument occurring and everyone involved was participating in this utter chaos? The scenario leaves you feeling tense and confused. Nobody knows what is going on. When you are dealing with irrational people it is difficult to find a resolution, as this is one continuous power struggle. Nobody wants to give up control and therefore nobody wants to believe the other person is right. There is no middle ground.

Compare this recollection with walking into a room filled with positive people. The room has an energy to it that is comfortable and enlightening. We feel at ease and not tense. The flow of energy is not stifled. One person gives and receives. There is a mutual giving and receiving of energy that is occurring. You don't have one person trying to declare control. Instead you have the group acting as a whole.

Often enough people don't pay attention or stop to recall these feelings and therefore numb their intuition and sometimes judgment to avoid any discomfort. When in fact in reality that discomfort we have when we go somewhere or are around certain people is for a reason. Our body and our mind are constantly working to let us know what is right for us and what is wrong. If we numb this intuition in ourselves, either through self-medication or over-indulgences such as unhealthy addictions, then we no longer can determine what is good for us and what is bad for us. Now granted, there are people walking around that are hindered by their own addictions that still make choices on a daily basis, but the difference between right and wrong becomes a fine line and harder to determine under these circumstances.

So what we have to do is retrain ourselves to think and retrain ourselves to feel. We can start by paying attention. When we enter any situation that involves other people, pay attention to how you feel when you are around them. Are you agitated? Are you feeling stressed? Are you feeling stifled like you can't think or feel for yourself? Or are you happy? Do you feel good being around certain people? Do you feel hopeful or do you feel miserable?

Sometimes people are delusional about what true happiness is as the definition changes depending on the person and the stage they are in their lives. What one person requires to be happy will not be the same as another person. And that is why it is so crucial for us to identify what makes us happy versus what someone tells us should make us happy.

If we spent our lives living the way someone else told us we should, then we wouldn't be living for ourselves and therefore our happiness would be lessened.

A perfect example is a woman who comes from a large family that never dates until she is out of high school and meets a man at work. She is ultimately encouraged by her family to make a long-term commitment to the relationship. They get married and have children, acquire financial obligations together such as cars and a house. Her family tells her what she should have her husband do, and she therefore influences what the husband does for a living.

The control of energy is passed from the family, to the woman, and she therefore places the end pressure on her husband, who now feels obligated to carry out her instructions for his life. They do this for 25 years of marriage, until one day the husband decides to leave her for another woman. He leaves because he declares he is not happy with the marriage.

Had both partners known initially what truly makes them happy as people, outsiders would have not influenced them so heavily. Instead of others having control over what makes two people happy, the couple may have had a better chance of maintaining the relationship or perhaps wouldn't have even carried out the relationship initially. So influence of others and what makes us happy can be two separate worlds.

Whether you are 20 years old or whether you are 60, age alone does not determine happiness. Happiness is not something we acquire with age; it is something we acquire through choice. When we strip ourselves away from others' influence of our happiness we start getting down to the core of what happiness is for us. We start asking the right questions and then seeking the right answers.

Nobody can determine for us what will make us happy, what will make us want to get up in the morning. Only we can decide and evaluate this. We have to find our happiness basically through trial and error. We have to experiment with life and see what feels right to us and what feels wrong. Again we are working through our own systems of checks and balances. We are finding the balance that feels right to us.

Nobody is raised perfect or lives perfectly, yet we do. We are already an item of perfection because of our own personal imperfections, as it is those same imperfections that provide others and us with the right tools we need to learn. Everyone has a certain gift that they are to unfold. Once we take time to develop our true purpose in life, we become happy. It is when we cover up who we are that we become agitated with life instead of hopeful.

Life isn't just about waking up in the morning, acquiring a job or place to go to, and then coming home only to repeat the cycle for the following day. We were intended to do more. We were intended to find more fulfillments in our lives than that. We are entitled to find personal gratification. Personal gratification makes us happy.

When we are not satisfied with ourselves or with other people we become miserable whether we realize it or not. When we become miserable, we begin to complain. For some, complaining is a way to release steam. We allow toxic thoughts to build up in our heads and then we release them. But what we don't realize is that we are releasing these toxic thoughts to the rest of the world, to the people close to us. We are essentially polluting others with our own words and negativity.

If every day you woke up and said, "Today is going to be a great day," then eventually you will convince yourself that this is the truth. And you know why this would become your truth? This thought would become your truth because you were actually consciously making it your truth.

No matter what the world can toss our way, whether it is grief, despair, or disease, we can face our day and start out with "Today is a good day." We can look at what we have in our hearts and around us instead of looking at what we have not. We can look at our glass half-full instead of half-empty.

As it is, our attitude alone creates our atmosphere. We can wake up and choose to be grateful; we can choose to be that which we were intended and deserve and that is to be happy.

If you are not happy, then you are not living life as you should be. Nobody was destined to live a life of unhappiness. Nobody is chosen to be lessened. We were all chosen to be of greatness, and in turn to be grateful for that greatness by sharing it with others.

What happens is we forget, we live our lives the way we have to in order to survive in the modern world. We have to financially support ourselves. We have to have a shelter over our heads and over our families' heads. We have to have food and clothing. These are needs that we constantly need to maintain. So we work. We might not enjoy what we have to do for work, but we are hopeful that some day we will not have to do the same work and that some day we will be able to do what we want.

But then what happens is time goes on and we forget what it was we wanted to do. Now we have acquired something more than what we had. Now we have placed not only needs in the forefront but also "wants." Now we are working for the nicer car, the nicer bikes, and the nicer computer. We become excessive instead of just working to secure our basic needs. Material items begin to take precedence in our lives as they provide a false sense of happiness to us.

People begin to replace personal gratification with material possessions. Instead of working harder and harder towards their initial goal that they wanted to accomplish, they begin to work harder and harder for an outside item whose gratification has a shelf life. This creates resentment instead of contentment. Soon we are buried in "things" instead of ambitions. Even a rich man can be simple if he chooses to be. The truth is we start to associate material items with happiness and we begin to believe that the more we have, the happier we will be. And for some they may feel this to be true temporarily until the newness wears off. Then they must quickly acquire another material item to compensate.

It is our nature to always want something. We do not have to complain about something that we wish to acquire that we placed a value on. Some people wish to win the lottery or to live in a big house. They wish they had this or that. When in actuality our focus should be on being happy right now, not wait for when we acquire that material item. Be happy in this moment and with this moment. Instead of saying "I will be happy when I have this..." we can say "I am happy with what I have at this moment."

Ultimately happiness comes down to one thing and one thing alone and that is yourself. If you are not happy with yourself you can basically forget everything else around you, including people, making you happy. It comes down to us. It comes down to our willingness to love who we are and where we are. It comes down to acceptance.

Not everyone loves his or her life situation. You might be going through a hard time in your life and feel that you are at your lowest point. That is when it is time to re-evaluate your personal earnings. We are not talking about finances. We are talking about our preciously earned life experiences. We are talking about our personal accomplishments. Some people always lessen themselves in this area, feeling as though they have not accomplished much in their lives.

When you start to evaluate your accomplishments make sure you are not comparing yourself with someone else. Everyone has a particular duty in life that they were intended to be earthbound to carry out. So comparing yourself and your accomplishments to another person's would not be a fair comparison. We need to narrow it down to ourselves. What have you done in your life that has made you feel accomplished? What are your greatest moments in your life? What are you proud of?

Feeling accomplished and reminding ourselves of these accomplishments is what adds longevity to our happiness. Feeling proud about what we have done with ourselves has a longevity that overrides what any material possession could ever have because it is something we carry with us; it is something we take with us wherever we go.

Take your journal out and start writing down your accomplishments. Then start writing down what you want or wish to accomplish. Start creating goals and writing them down so you can visually remind yourself of them. Some people accomplish a lot in their lives early on and some people accomplish more as they get older. Everyone is different and we have to understand that. If you were not motivated to accomplish a goal that would ultimately make you happy, then start doing so now. It is never too late to carry out your goals. It is never too late to actually sit down and write down goals that are in your reach. We don't have to settle for less.

We don't have to do the same thing for the rest of our lives. We don't have to stay in bad life situations. We don't have to complain about a life we have control over. Granted there are a lot of things in life that we do not have control over and those are other people, places, and things. However, the one thing we do have control over is ourselves. We can be good to ourselves and as a result be good to other people. We can be happy.

If you are not currently happy or overjoyed in your life then you need to sit down and look at why this is the case. What are you discontent with? What areas in your life do you feel overburdened by or feel you need to change? By taking a good look at your unhappiness and the cause for this unhappiness, you are bringing the issue into your awareness. Awareness is the most powerful and overwhelming feeling anyone can ever have or acquire. It is that feeling that we experience when we stand alone without blinders on. It is when we can see ourselves in our own truth and therefore see others in that truth as well. We won't always like what we see, but the gift of having that sight alone, is a powerful induction to change.

Once you have written down what you are unhappy with, go back and put a checkmark on any particular item that is related to material items. For example if you have on your list that you are unhappy with where you are living and want a new house or apartment, go ahead and checkmark that item on your list. We will not say wanting perhaps a new house or moving into a new apartment is a negative reason for unhappiness, as our environment can affect our outlook on our lives, but just check the items that are related to material gain so you can see where you are with your own discontentment.

Personal satisfaction and contentment are something we can acquire without finances. When you put a check on the items that are relating to financial acquiring or success, we are going to see how much of your happiness is actually depending on money versus actual personal change. What we are ultimately trying to do here is to eliminate the "if I had more" attitude that many of us can become plagued by. There are always going to be the "If I had this..." mentality but we can try our best to recognize this and work around it. Instead of the "If I had more..." our goal is to say, "I have what I need for right now."

When we say this we are basically telling ourselves that we are okay with what we have. We may need more in the future, but we are okay with what we have right now. Right now is all we have. We have this moment. Yesterday is far behind and tomorrow is far ahead; for what we have in this moment is today.

Make your happiness a priority today. Sometimes we can be so overly concerned with others' well-being that we forget about our own. So if this is the case for you, acknowledge this behavior and write it down in your journal. Remember we cannot control other people, places, or things. This being known, that means that someone else's well-being is not something we can control. Children and elderly loved ones are exceptions to this rule if we are their primary care givers. But fully capable adults are not our responsibility.

We have the right to be happy. We also have a right to take time out for ourselves and find what makes us happy. Our happiness also affects those around us so it is crucial for us to know where we are in our lives and where we want to be.

For some people, this may mean taking time to slow down our pace and not always run to the finish line. Set realistic goals for yourself and allow yourself to feel the power of personal achievements when you reach those goals. You will know something is right by the way you feel. You will know something makes you happy when you smile without effort.

Journal Exercise 5

1. What have you done in your life that has made you feel accomplished? What are your greatest moments in your life? What are you proud of?

2. Start writing down what you want or wish to accomplish. Start creating goals and writing them down so you can visually remind yourself of them.

3. Once you have written down what you are unhappy with, go back and put a checkmark on any particular item that is related to material items. For example if you have on your list that you are unhappy with where you are living and want a new house or apartment, go ahead and checkmark that item on your list. We will not say wanting perhaps a new house or moving into a new apartment is a negative reason for unhappiness, as our environment can affect our outlook on our lives, but just check the items that are related to material gain so you can see where you are with your own discontentment.

4. Write down realistic goals for yourself that involve personal achievement and that do not depend on other people.

Chapter 6
accepting
CHANGE

Old shoes tend to fit us quite nicely. They feel good and we know what to expect out of them, hence we are reluctant to throw them away or buy new shoes. The same theory applies to our own lives when we face the opportunity to make a change. We don't always accept change or view it as a catalyst to move forward. Instead we might feel challenged by change and even reluctant to accept what the change has to offer us.

People get used to complaining; they get accustomed to feeling miserable and so anything other than this is virtually unknown to them. Imagine people spending over half their lives complaining, then one day they are presented with the challenge to change the way they have been living up to this point. They would feel awkward and out of their own element. Doing something different challenges their everyday routine. A lot of time is wasted on complaining, so if someone was to stop complaining or catch themselves when they do complain, they might not know what to do with the extra time they have in their lives.

In our previous chapters we discuss awareness being the key to our overall success with change. We can't change anything about ourselves unless we are aware of what it is we are doing and need to change. Once you have awareness, you can then cross over to acceptance. You can accept yourself and then work towards changing the things you don't feel are your strong points in life.

Now it is time to go back and look at your first journal entry where you listed the items that you complain about on a daily basis. Re-read what you wrote and then mark them with a number to mark importance, #1 being the most important, #4 or so on being of least importance.

Out of the list, what is present that you have control over? What is on your list that you do not have control over or is not your responsibility to begin with? Our goal is to minimize complaining and the time we waste doing it, creating more time for other valuable goals that need to be addressed. If there is something making you that miserable that you find yourself being preoccupied with it at all times, then it is time to initiate a change.

Maybe you are unhappy with your job, your relationship, or your location. Whatever it is, take a realistic look at the unhappiness and discontentment you feel that it has caused you. If something causes us more grief than it does happiness, then we need to look at why we choose to have it in our lives or be a part of it.

Now there are some circumstances that cause us grief but are naturally a phase of our relationships that do require our presence. Maybe a loved one is ill and needs our support. Even if the situation might cause us grief, we are still unconditionally caring for the person and want to support them through their hard times.

However, there are moments when we inadvertently are not required to be involved in a dramatic situation, but choose to be. This often affects our outlooks and can even take away needed energy to accomplish tasks that make us happy. So what we are doing when we overstep our bounds and involve ourselves in an emotionally draining situation, we are actually subtracting from the time we have to spend on a task that allows us to feel accomplished about ourselves.

Don't assume that other people will assist you with your goals in your life. Assume that this is your responsibility and yours alone. Granted some people may come into your life and help you along the way, but be willing to accomplish your goals whether people will support you or not. Be willing to make a change in your life whether people support that change or not.

Just as you are likely scared of change, so are those around you that will be impacted by the change itself. When we start to correct our own imperfections, it also forces others to look a little closer at their own actions and people don't always want to support that. In fact they may do anything they can to prevent the change from occurring.

Some people that are close to you will appreciate the change and some will not. Some people will stand by you and others will walk away. Know that for what is lost there will always be more gained. When one door closes, another door opens. We have to be willing to let go in order to gain. We have to be willing to remove the people, places, and things in our lives that no longer fit our goals or ambitions. Let change begin with you.

When we hold on to burdens we are essentially holding on to an anchor that will keep us from becoming that which we were intended. The tighter we hold on the longer we are going to continue to stay at the bottom. It is when we are willing to let go that we will float to the top.

We provide the most for other people when we provide for ourselves. We always think the opposite is true; however our happiness reflects onto others. We are able to feel more giving and more caring, and more loving to those we encounter when we ourselves are stemming from a place inside ourselves that we are content with.

If we are miserable and unhappy then we don't feel much like being around people, let alone wanting to share ourselves with them. If we are around them we may spread our agitation more than we spread happiness.

Often people fear making a change because they might think it is too selfish of them to make. Perhaps they fear investing time in themselves when they think they should be focusing on others' lives and helping them.

For example, let's picture a farmer that has several crops that are successful. He is so successful that other farmers begin to request his assistance. He is complimented by the success being acknowledged and also wants to help others with harvesting their crops. What happens is that the successful farmer ends up putting so much energy into other people's farms that he is late on planting and harvesting his own fields. As a result he doesn't earn the money he needs to continue farming. His success becomes his failure.

We have to know our own limitations and boundaries when it comes to investing our energy into other people and situations. Helping people is always a very noble idea, but we also have to be willing to help ourselves. It's okay to focus on yourself. It's okay to pay attention to our needs and address our goals. By practicing taking our own personal inventory, we stop complaining so much about others and look towards ourselves for some much needed evaluations.

We start focusing on changing ourselves and not others. Did you ever know someone that spends all their time complaining about other people? What type of lives do they have? Maybe you never noticed them before or maybe you didn't pay attention to their own well-being that was affected. Often times the people that are complaining the most about others are people that need the most personal evaluations performed.

However, people run; they run away from themselves and as long as they continue to focus on other people they consume so much time that they use it for an excuse not to take care of themselves. The cycle continues over and over. The person distances themselves away from their own truth.

There is a difference between helping out others and using our helping mechanisms as a form of avoidance of our own goals. Perhaps initially we have the goal within our reach and in our minds, but then we start to become occupied by either other people or responsibilities and never fully seek the resolution of accomplishing the goal. We keep placing our goal on the backburner until one day we are so distant from our ambitions that they go overlooked.

A primary example is a man or a woman that has an aspiration to become successful in an art. Art by all means is not an instant success and it takes a great deal of time and effort to become successful in the field. Let's say this person starts a family and primary goals switch from art to providing for a family. The caregiver has a priority that they cannot avoid. This priority becomes a necessity.

However, the person does not have to give up their goal of becoming or working on their art. Granted their time may be consumed on acquiring finances for the family, but the overall goal does not have to go overlooked. Sometimes when we feel we cannot dedicate all of our time to one particular goal, instead of putting in some effort we may not put in any effort at all. This alone can become our downfall.

We have goals and desires for a reason. We develop passions and our zest for life because we are supposed to. When we look at all of the factors of our lives and how change has unfolded onto us, we will begin to see that when we accept change, we are accepting a metamorphosis that allows ourselves to not only see our goals differently, but also be more focused on acquiring them.

Our first task was to eliminate useless time spent on complaining. Our second task was eliminating the negative. Our third task asks us to look at change and accept it. Breaking old patterns is considered change. Stopping ourselves from complaining without action is a change. Stopping ourselves from participating in negative people's lives is a huge change.

If you have never focused inward and are doing so now, this is a change, and a well-needed one. We can't live our lives for others. If we do, we are going to base our happiness on others' expectations of us versus the expectations we have set for ourselves.

Change can be awkward and for some it can be very frightening, but it doesn't have to be. We can recall when we were younger, our body and our minds were changing all the time. We would have growing pains through different stages of our lives. Our lives now are no different; when change is invited into our world we can expect to go through some moments of awkwardness and discomfort, not just because of our own fear of uncertainty, but also because of our fear of transformation.

We spend a lifetime searching for answers and then we soon realize that as we grow the questions change.

Let's take this moment to start writing down what has changed within ourselves up to this point we are at in our lives. You don't have to write about every single change you ever had in your life; just note changes you felt that bettered you as a person.

The more we are able to see the positive effects of change in our lives, the more we are going to be willing to invite change instead of fearing it.

Once you have written down the major changes that have occurred in your life, then take a moment to think of the changes you want to make currently. This is a good time to write about uncertainties you might have with your future.

After you have completed these two entries then you can sit down and write about your course for action. What do you want to change right now if you could? Would you change your appearance, your attitude, your goals, or the people you surround yourself with? Maybe you would prefer to change your job or acquire something that is more in line with your aspirations. Maybe you want to change bad habits that you have and better yourself. Write down what you want to change and then write down how you can change. Write down your course of action. Visualize yourself achieving the goal and write down the steps you need to accomplish this.

If you have fears, write them down and work through them. Sometimes seeing everything on paper in black and white allows us to organize our thoughts and see them for what they really are. We have nothing to be afraid of; fear need not be a hindrance to us.

Instead of running from change, we can begin accepting change and welcoming it.

Journal Exercise 6

1. Now it is time to go back and look at your first journal entry where you listed the items that you complain about on a daily basis. Re-read what you wrote and then mark them with a number to mark importance, #1 being the most important, #4 or so on being of least importance.

2. Out of the list, what is present that you have control over? What is on your list that you do not have control over or is not your responsibility to begin with?

3. Start writing down what has changed within ourselves up to this point we are at in our lives. You don't have to write about every single change you ever had in your life; just note changes you felt that bettered you as a person.

4. Once you have written down the major changes that have occurred in your life, then take a moment to think of the changes you want to make currently. This is a good time to write about uncertainties you might have with your future.

5. After you have completed these two entries then you can sit down and write about your course for action. What do you want to change right now if you could? Would you change your appearance, your attitude, your goals, or the people you surround yourself with? Maybe you would prefer to change your job or acquire something that is more in line with your aspirations. Maybe you want to change bad habits that you have and better yourself. Write down what you want to change and then write down how you can change. Write down your course of action. Visualize yourself achieving the goal and write down the steps you need to accomplish this. If you have any fears on making these changes, write those down as well.

Chapter 7
just say THANK YOU

Everyone has their own ways of dealing with compliments from other people. We can start out with first listening to how we talk about ourselves. Are we quick to correct someone that tries to compliment us? Or are we quick to say thank you. Depending on where you are with yourself will interpret your answers.

If you don't feel you deserve the compliment you will be very quick with someone to let them know you yourself do not believe in the praise you are being provided with. Instead of acknowledging the praise you confirm your own beliefs and weaknesses by giving yourself a verbal cue that actually cancels out the compliment.

Someone is trying to reciprocate positive energy to you and instead of you accepting this, you are repelling by expressing your own self-doubts and feeling of unworthiness. Sure, no one wants to have people think they are overly-confident of themselves. Nobody wants others to think that we are built out of ego alone.

However, it is our lack of self-esteem that determines the type of energy we draw to ourselves and to other people. If we give off negative energy, then a lot of the times that is what we wind up attracting. If we feel bad about ourselves then we can tend to wind up in bad situations or relations. When we feel confident about ourselves and feel good about ourselves we are placing more of a focus on who we are and our values. We will want to be around positive people most of the time as this is what furthers our positive energy.

Positivity makes you feel good; it makes you feel hopeful about your future and your present being. When we reaffirm our self-worth we are actually telling ourselves that we have a future worth containing and striving towards. We are willing to say that we ourselves have a value that no other person, place, or thing can place upon us. We are giving ourselves our own currency of worth.

Ideally not every day can we always be positive or have a positive outlook on our life. The reality is that there are always going to be challenging situations that will present an obstacle to our positive selves. Our goal, however, is no matter what the day may bring, to say two simple words: "thank you."

If someone gives you a compliment, say "thank you." Even if you don't believe the comment yourself, say those words. Don't counteract them with your own negative thoughts. Don't restrict them or limit their presentation to you or interrupt the person giving them; just listen, and say "thank you."

This might sound like the simplest rule to follow but for some of you this will be a great challenge. Depending on what type of foundation you are stemming from or whether or not your self-esteem has already been scarred, this will certainly affect the outcome.

Sometimes we just need to act the part we wish to play in life. If we are negative or feel awkward, then we can act as though we are positive and feel confident. Eventually our mind and body will follow along with our self-portrayal.

Once we practice saying the words, "thank you," we will soon overcome our need to dispute praise. We might even begin to accept the fact that we have earned our place in this world and deserve to be recognized for it.

We have to rise above our own fear of self worth and accept ourselves as is and then accept ourselves as a constant state of becoming. We have control over what burdens we wish to carry. We have control over the relationships we choose to invite.

We have control over the words that come from our mouths and whether we speak negatively or positively towards ourselves. We have the ability to rebuild, renew, and recharge ourselves when needed and we have every right to do so.

Will every compliment that someone delivers to us be sincere? No, of course not. Not everyone walks on the path of truth; but either way a compliment is a compliment and sometimes can be an enlightening reflection of ourselves that was never revealed to us, and hence we should always listen to his or her delights.

Not only should you be saying "thank you" to others, but you should also be saying "thank you" to yourself both verbally and nonverbally. When we treat ourselves right we are quietly saying thank you to ourselves. We are telling ourselves that we are worth the effort and the energy to maintain.

Think how often we care for others on a daily basis and never return the favor to ourselves. Perhaps we are limited on time or feel we are a lesser responsibility than others and therefore neglect to prioritize ourselves in the equation. It is important that we always set time for ourselves to do whatever we feel is needed to better or nurture ourselves.

We never know what talent is lurking until we actually give ourselves time to develop our skills. And if you don't feel good about yourself you usually don't feel like devoting extra effort into talents that might actually benefit you and others. Instead of implementing change or furthering our greatness we end up being our own handicap.

Self-confidence can make every difference in the world when we approach ourselves. Our lack of confidence can actually deter our success by leaps and bounds, because we stop ourselves dead in our tracks. We wind up losing the race before it even began. Failure happens in the mind first and in the world second.

It is when we stop believing in ourselves that we forget our goals and desires as we learn to put them on the back burner. We continue on in the world knowing that something inside of us is hidden and not revealed. We might ignore our talents and our gifts for so long that we actually convince ourselves that they no longer exist.

The result comes in a dissatisfaction of the heart, a longing for something we cannot explain but only feel. This internal grief can become a burden carried for years and years until we are willing to unleash our desires and our purpose and fulfill our life's intention.

We can never run from this. We can avoid who we are, we can avoid what we are, but in time it will find us right back where we should have started in the first place. Part of living a life of gratitude starts by living the way we were intended to be living. If you are doing something you don't want to be doing, or feel is not your path in life, then you will never be satisfied.

What results is that you are creating your own friction between the life you live and the life you want to live.

The dissatisfaction comes out in agitation, grief, and hidden anger. It becomes an imbalance due to the internal restrictions that we have placed upon ourselves. This becomes a roadblock instead of what we should have created: a path. Everyone wants to feel good at something. We want to feel the subtle rewards for our daily efforts. We want to feel that what we have accomplished today had reaped some sort of pinnacle.

If we are not feeling this sense of fulfillment, we are only creating a world in which we are dissatisfied with and that causes a world in which we complain more often than live. Instead of becoming a part of our own solution we become a part of the problem.

Our goal is to rebuild our confidence and our faith in ourselves. We can start out small and take baby steps and build ourselves back up to a healthy confidence level.

When we are referring to non-verbal and verbal cues of saying "thank-you," we are not just referring to what other people say to us out loud; we are also referring to what we say to ourselves without any words at all. Are we holding our heads up high or are we crouched down and staring at the floor?

What postures do we have? Are we limp and just not poised at all? Are we neat in our appearance or are we sloppy? Are we clean or are we dirty? Are we maintained or just thrown together? Are we organized or are we constantly in disarray? All of these questions may seem to be mundane or non-important but at the same time, they are non-verbal cues that are telling ourselves daily whether we care for ourselves or not.

You might be a very loving mother or father and do the world for others, but when it comes to yourself, you could care less. And sure you might think what is wrong with that? Well, there is a lot wrong with that as our loved ones want to see us happy just as much as we want them to be happy. And when we forget to send some of our loving and caring ways over to ourselves it is essentially saying that we do not feel we are worth the effort or added energy.

There are little baby steps that we can take to better ourselves and show ourselves our own gratitude. Are you eating properly? Are you getting enough rest? Are you drinking enough water? Are you taking time out of your day to spend on something you enjoy alone? We should never disregard the little things, for the little things can add up to become a big part of the problem of self-defeat if disregarded.

Are you exercising your mind and your body? If anything is imbalanced in our body, then it causes an imbalance in our mind. We don't always make the best judgments when we are tired or we are hungry. We might be hasty in our decision-making or feel a sense or urgency, as there is an imbalance that is demanding more of our attention.

Did you ever go to an office right before lunchtime and try to get someone to accomplish something for you? You might have encountered some negativity or felt rushed when you spoke to the people. What you were feeling was the imbalance that they were giving off. They have a need that is demanding their attention more so than their job.

We have to listen to these non-verbal cues in our bodies so that we can always give ourselves what we need. If we are hungry, eat. If we are thirsty, drink. If we are tired, then we need to sleep. Listening to our bodies, we will learn to listen and develop our confidence and work with ourselves instead of against ourselves.

We can certainly be our worst enemy when it comes to showing care for ourselves. We might find more excuses than reasons to place time and effort on building our foundations, but we need to. If we constantly put ourselves last, it will wind up catching up with us and become even more difficult to return back to normal. Again, this will leave us feeling dissatisfied and unaccomplished. When we are left feeling a sense of inadequacy, we end up feeling as though we are burdened more than feeling enlightened and enriched as we were intended.

We need to spend that personal time to get ourselves to return to a balance. Maybe you enjoy reading a good book or journaling and writing about what you learned throughout the day. Little things that we put attention towards that help us better ourselves can go a long way. Subtle attention to our fine lines and details can make the difference between depression and success.

Dress the part and feel good about portraying that confidence. What happens is when we start investing in ourselves we start feeling the way we were intended to feel: successful. We start feeling as though we are no longer bounded by ourselves. We feel lighter and we feel less burdened.

Just like negative energy is contagious, so is positive energy. We can actually benefit those around us by investing in ourselves as our confidence in our abilities exudes from us and is projected onto others.

The only way we can examine our own gratitude towards others and ourselves is to get our journals out and start writing it down. So first start out with your main topic. Write down "Thank-you," at the very top of your page, then separate your page into two columns. Mark down the first column "Others" and then the second column is going to be called "Self."

The first column, "Others" is for you to begin marking down what compliments from others you may have received. Don't worry about time frame on this exercise. It could be a compliment that was told to you as a child or a compliment that was given to you recently. Just the mere fact that you remember a compliment expresses the importance and impact it placed on you.

Also note your response to the person that gave you the compliment. How did you feel when they complimented you? What was your reaction? How did you respond to their praise?

Now go into your second column and write down what forms of gratitude you provide to yourself. How do you tell yourself you are thankful? What positive things or habits do you carry out for yourself? What time do you invest in yourself? How do you show praise to yourself?

Now take out another sheet of paper and start writing down any negative comments you receive. Make a column that says "Others" and another that says "Self." What negative comments have you received from people? Again, do not place a timeframe on this exercise. Write about anything that affected you, any comments that might have felt damaging to you.

When you are done, start writing down negative thoughts and/or actual actions that you imposed on yourself. Negative thoughts alone have energy to them, so it is important to give attention to our negative thoughts so that we can address them appropriately.

Feel free to use more paper if you need to or make additional pages if necessary. The point of this exercise is for you to see where your confidence level is and also to see what might be having a negative effect on you. If one column outweighs the other, if you see that others are giving you praise more than yourself, then you need to start looking at different ways that you can give yourself some attention. What changes can you make to adjust this?

Also evaluate your responses to people giving you praise. Were you confident in accepting their compliments or were you refusing their compliment with your own rebuttal?

Then take a look at negative thoughts that have come up from others and yourself. Evaluate how you felt when you heard these comments or had these thoughts about yourself. What type of action would you take in the future if you had more confidence or solidified yourself as a person? Would you respond differently to people? Would you recover quicker from your own thoughts of despair?

As a special note, anyone that has had thoughts about harming themselves or other people should seek professional attention. If you feel you or others are endangered please contact your local hotlines found in your local phonebook, usually under the government listings.

Negative thoughts can lead to negative actions so that is why it is always crucial to address these issues appropriately. Doing so can save our own lives and prevent unnecessary harm to others. If you have an addiction that needs to be addressed, there is help available to you; it is just a matter of reaching out to the right people in your area.

Don't be surprised if you begin having emotions while you are writing down these exercises. In fact, look at any emotions you begin to experience and graciously accept them. Let them purge out of you and don't give them a label. Just allow these thoughts and feelings to be released.

When we have any unused energy that stays inside of us, we store it and it builds up just like any energy would. Eventually this energy has to come to the surface. So it is better to release this energy willingly then to try to continue to suppress its presence.

Journal Exercise 7

1. The only way we can examine our own gratitude towards others and ourselves is to get our journals out and start writing it down. So first start out with your main topic. Write down "Thank-you," at the very top of your page and then separate your page into two columns. Mark down the first column "Others" and then the second column is going to be called "Self."

The first column, "Others," is for you to begin marking down what compliments from others you may have received. Don't worry about time frame on this exercise. It could be a compliment that was told to you as a child or a compliment that was given to you recently. Just the mere fact that you remember a compliment expresses the importance and impact it placed on you.

Also note your response to the person that gave you the compliment. How did you feel when they complimented you? What was your reaction? How did you respond to their praise?

2. Now go into your second column and write down what forms of gratitude you provide to yourself. How do you tell yourself you are thankful? What positive things or habits do you carry out for yourself? What time do you invest in yourself? How do you show praise to yourself?

3. Now take out another sheet of paper and start writing down any negative comments you receive. Make a column that says "Others" and another that says "Self." What negative comments have you received from people? Again, do not place a timeframe on this exercise. Write about anything that affected you, any comments that might have felt damaging to you.

4. When you are done, start writing down negative thoughts and or actual actions that you imposed on yourself. Negative thoughts alone have energy to them, so it is important to give attention to our negative thoughts so that we can address them appropriately.

5. Evaluate your responses to people giving you praise. Were you confident in accepting their compliments or

were you refusing their compliment with your own rebuttal?

6. Then take a look at negative thoughts that have come up from others and yourself. Evaluate how you felt when you heard these comments or had these thoughts about yourself. What type of action would you take in the future if you had more confidence or solidified yourself as a person? Would you respond differently to people? Would you recover quicker from your own thoughts of despair?

Chapter 8

breaking the HABIT

Bad habits are hard to break, especially when for some of us complaining becomes a daily ritual. We might not even realize how often we participate in this activity, let alone how much complaining consumes our lives, until we are literally exhausted by it or exhausted from listening to others complaints.

A complainer always seeks something to be wrong instead of something to be right. So with that in mind we can predict that a complainer is viewing the world around them in a pessimistic way instead of an opportunist. An opportunist views the world as always an opportunity even if that opportunity isn't made known to them at the current moment. They go on the premise that more in life will be revealed and that there is purpose in this moment whether they can identify that or not.

This is where the laws of gravity and trust come into play. We have to be willing to trust something we do not see or hear. We have to be willing to let go and allow the universe to indicate a balance to us when rightfully time to do so. Does this mean we will have our answers to a certain predicament right away? No. It merely means that we agree that the issue is there and that a solution will be made known to us when it is appropriate, and complaining about the situation will only cause more burden than relief.

If complaining about something in your life causes more of a burden then relief, then it is unnecessary. If it is a complaint without action, then we are consciously making a decision to stay in a situation that we're not pleased with.

When we choose this sort of self-defeating discomfort we are continuing a life pattern that will exist as long as we do. We have to at some point decide that we want to be more involved with our own happiness and that we want to break some of the patterns we keep finding ourselves involved in.

If something is a reoccurring theme in your life, for example you feel that you are constantly being presented with situations where you are an active enabler, or you keep involving yourself with unhealthy relationships, then this is an active life pattern for you. You have to identify this, discover why you feel you keep involving yourself in these situations, and then find the root of the cause.

We can break the habit. We can have the pattern stop with us. We do not have to keep going in a circle, only finding ourselves right back where we started. If you begin seeing a reoccurring theme surface in your life over and over, then that is when it is time to put on the brakes and stop. Instead of taking action, it is time to take a moment of inaction and look at where you are going before you just start trying to go forward.

It is like a person that is traveling to an unknown territory. They realize they are lost, but they keep driving instead of stopping to ask for directions. Life is no different; if you keep driving when you are already lost, you can't expect to find your way blindly. Instead, stop and ask for directions and give yourself time to listen and observe before taking action.

Some people like drama in their lives and feed off of it. They simply migrate from one drama to the next. Some even go as far as creating dramas that do not even exist. They develop an idea in their head and actually convince themselves that their theories are true and then they actually tell others these falsehoods, which breed even more drama.

There are a lot of factors that can inhibit drama. Some people are more prone than others to be drawn to these dramatic reenactments and are therefore deeply affected by their inclusion in their lives.

For example, we will refer to a dramatic that wakes up and watches the news a couple times a day.

They don't just watch the weather; they watch all the dramatic events that occur over the world, most of which are reporting a tragedy or chaos. The news embeds an outlook of the world to the end-user and that user carries this over to their day-by-day activities.

They may have initially felt hopeful about their day, but now after watching tragic events on a daily basis they are beginning to have self-doubt, as the "problem" is too massive for one to burden themselves with trying to initiate a change. This person might respond outwardly to the world with panic instead of ease, which spreads the drama instead of keeping it isolated.

So if you are finding yourself being influenced by something in your immediate surroundings that is causing you to feel doubt in your life and the world around you, then do what you can to either limit the use or take a vacation from it altogether.

There is nothing wrong with turning the television off and taking a break from reading the newspaper. Our goal is to focus on breaking the habits of complainers, so instead of focusing on the worldly events that we do not have immediate control over, we can focus our attention back on ourselves.

We want to eliminate the time we spend complaining and we also want to eliminate the time we spend even "watching" others complain. With the boom of reality television, other people's complaints and dramas have become our own. We are no longer just watching actors. Instead we are watching what we believe are real people placed in real situations that can cause drama.

So as you are exploring the possible causes for your complaining, look at all the daily rituals you perform and see where there is excess. Take out a piece of paper and actually write down what you do all day and the hours you spend doing it. Are you watching television all night? What are you watching? Are you watching a lot of dramatizations that might have an impact on how you resolve or deal with your own life issues?

How much of the news are you exposing yourself to? Are you spending your time watching movies with drama? Are you spending your time exposing yourself to other people with dramas and trying to find solutions for them? If so, how many hours are you dedicating to this?

Break everything down and itemize it like you would an invoice, as this is your time you are spending but not being compensated for. When you are done, take a good look at where most of your time is going. Are you using your time wisely? Or are you wasting your time? Do you see any places where you can eliminate hours spent on doing a certain task?

Where we spend our free time outside of work is crucial to our well-being. Are you doing something that is constructive or are you doing something that is destructive? Are you doing something that will benefit you as a person or are you doing something that is inhibiting your growth?

Once you have a proper assessment of your time, you can work on eliminating factors that may cause you to feel less dissatisfied and more satisfied. The happier we are with our lives, the less we will feel the need to complain. So our goal is to lessen the stresses, whether environmental or self-inflicted, and increase the activities that provide us with overall well-being.

If you are not happy, write down why you feel this way. If you don't know, then write that down too. It's okay to sit down and admit that you do not know something. It is okay to admit that you do not have an answer to a life question, as there will always be times when we don't have the answers.

Just the mere fact that you are willing to write it all down says that you are willing to seek the answers and that is when awareness alone will come into play. Sometimes we don't realize everything that we have going on around us or in our worlds until we stop to write about it. That is why during our times of uncertainty it is invaluable to write down our thoughts and emotions and sort through them with a fine-tooth comb. Dissect your thoughts. Dissect your life situations and look at them closely, as if you were viewing them under a magnifying glass.

We don't always have to stay in analytical mode, but there are times when it is good to turn on this switch in ourselves so we can look at ourselves more clearly. Let us see ourselves in a different light so that we can make corrections and alterations where needed.

Sometimes we are fortunate to have people close to us point out our troubled areas so we can look at them more closely and decide what validity these comments have on us. Are we really like that? Do we really act in that way? These questions are certainly helpful to ask yourself when you are making an assessment. We don't want you to torment yourself too hard, but do understand there is always discomfort that may result in your reality depending on just where you are in your life.

If you keep an open mind to this process you will find that any discomfort you happen to experience during this period will only be temporary, but the benefits you will encounter will stay with you for a lifetime. You have to be willing to take that step, break the habits and move on from that point. You can start over any time you choose to and that is the beauty of life. We can pick ourselves up from off the ground when we decide we have had enough of living life one way and we can move forward.

Change will always come to those willing to seek its presence.

Journal Exercise 8

1. So as you are exploring the possible causes for your complaining, look at all the daily rituals you perform and see where there is excess. Take out a piece of paper and actually write down what you do all day and the hours you spend doing it. Are you watching television all night? What are you watching? Are you watching a lot of dramatizations that might have an impact on how you resolve or deal with your own life issues?

2. How much of the news are you exposing yourself to? Are you spending your time watching movies with drama? Are you spending your time exposing yourself to other people with dramas and trying to find solutions for them? If so, how many hours are you dedicating to this?

3. Break everything down and itemize it like you would an invoice, as this is your time you are spending but not being compensated for. When you are done, take a good look at where most of your time is going. Are you using your time wisely? Or are you wasting

your time? Do you see any places where you can eliminate hours spent on doing a certain task?

4. Where we spend our free time outside of work is crucial to our well-being. Are you doing something that is constructive or are you doing something that is destructive? Are you doing something that will benefit you as a person or are you doing something that is inhibiting your growth.

5. If you are not happy, write down why you feel this way. If you don't know, then write that down too. It's okay to sit down and admit that you do not know something. It is okay to admit that you do not have an answer to a life question, as there will always be times when we don't have the answers.

Chapter 9

justified COMPLAINING

If you complain about your job for example, break it down to sizable bites and analyze what it is that you are not feeling satisfied with. Is it the tasks, the time you have to spend performing the job, or is it the compensation? What can you do to change your dissatisfaction? You can work towards finding another job or you can address the issues with your current employer and see if they are willing to meet you halfway on some of your needs that you feel are not being addressed. This is where complaining can be made constructive instead of destructive. Of course addressing your concerns to an employer also imposes a risk, as it would to anyone that we expressed our opinions towards.

The other party can always refuse our requests or deny them as they have such a right. However, if you weigh out your options, taking a risk can sometimes be a benefit and be a catalyst for growth; we just have to choose our battles wisely. If complaining might do more harm than good, we have to wage that out. Know when to speak and when not to speak.

Are we complaining out of ego alone or are we complaining because we feel we deserve to and we need a change to compensate for our additional efforts? It is okay to take risks but take a calculated risk, meaning make sure you think through different scenarios prior to taking an action. Position yourself first and then once you have achieved as much as you can then take your action.

Sometimes we do not have everything we need to make a validated argument towards something or someone else. If you just started working somewhere,, for example, and you approached the Manager and inquired about gaining an Assistant Manager position then they would likely say "no" because you have not learned everything there is to learn about the scope of the business. You have to know when you are prepared to advance before you seek the advancement.

Even with relationships that we have, if we ran out and asked the first person we were ever with to marry us, we might not be ready for the responsibility that marriage entails. We might overstep our bounds and actually scare away the other party involved due to our own haste.

Timing is a necessity. We have to earn our experience and our knowledge and then graduate to different advancements in our life. Everyone starts out on the bottom. Overnight successes are few and far between. They do exist but they are rare and that is often due to seniority levels.

So what exactly is "justified" complaining? Complaints that have validity and are not performed simply out of malice are considered to be justified. Some people might actually term this as "venting."

Have you ever had a hard day at work and you come home or end your day and you just feel awful? Maybe something happened that didn't make you feel good at all and you needed to go home and talk about it to someone. This would be considered justified complaining. There is nothing wrong with getting our feelings off our chest in a safe arena with someone we trust and feel comfortable with. Not only does the conversation usually make us feel better when we are finished, but it also makes the weight we feel on us a little lighter.

We may gain a new perspective on ourselves and our role in the discomfort that we feel. Or we may learn how to actually try and work better with others instead of working against them. Some people have a lot of difficulty working with people that are above rank with them. They might have trouble with authority figures and not desire working for other people but have to because of financial situations.

The most important understanding that we can have is that we do not have to do something forever. If we put this theory into perspective and repeat those words daily to ourselves, then we can adapt the concept that the work we have to do right now is only temporary and we can seek to better our situation when it comes time to do so.

We do not have to feel restricted or limited by our "jobs," as long as we always strive towards bettering ourselves to acquire the goals that we wish to seek. We can make all of our ideal purposes in life a reality.

Nothing goes to waste here. No experience that you acquire during this moment will go wasted. Will you realize this right now? Will you realize the value years from now? One can never tell, but know that this moment alone will benefit you in the future.

If we view our lives as purposeful then we can view our discomforts as beneficial. We can do a task that we don't enjoy doing a little longer because we know that we do not have to do it forever. We can take pride in this moment and know that it serves a purpose for right now.

You may not like your job, but it serves the purpose you need it to: food, shelter, and clothing. You may not like going to school, but it will serve the purpose you intend it to later on in life. You may not like where you are physically, but you know that when the opportunity for you to relocate is supposed to happen it will happen.

So when we have justified complaints to someone that we trust, we can essentially be thinking out loud. Some of the greatest light bulbs can go off in our heads when we actually repeat the situation we are having issues with to another person.

When we are complaining about a relationship that we have with another person, the subject can tend to get a little more personal. Relationships are not something that we just spend 8 or 9 hours a day on and come home like a job; instead relationships can be very intense and involved. If you live with the person then you are around them more frequently and will not seem to get a break to look at the situation more clearly.

Relationships are very difficult to detach from because they affect us physically and emotionally. Due to the fact that a real person is involved and not just a physical job, we feel more apt to show a loyalty to someone we have placed a lot of effort into. We feel devoted to someone and can become fearful of making needed changes.

So when we are expressing our dissatisfaction with our current partners to another person this can be very helpful to us as we are speaking to someone that is distant from the situation. Nobody can be as close to a situation as we are. Having someone that is a neutral party can help us identify potential harmful cases in a relationship and that is why justified complaining can take form into a needed action.

Sometimes when we are looking too closely at a situation that we are involved in we can't see all the details. Imagine taking an apple and holding it up to your eye as close as you can. What will you see? Will you see all the fine details of the apple? Will you see the intricate shades of red that are a part of the skin? Will you be able to make out the shape of the apple? No, you will only see a red blur.

Viewing our relationships with people is very similar, as we will only see the details when we step back from the relationship itself and then take a look. And even then we can run into issues as we are still personally attached to the situation. When we discuss our relationships with another person we trust we can uncover a lot of realities about the partnership.

Maybe we are not being treated as we should be but we don't realize that because we do not have healthy relationships to compare them to. So when we discuss unhealthy occurrences in the relationship with someone else we might be able to get another perspective from someone and therefore have insight on the relationship itself.

For anyone in a potentially harmful relationship this is a very important step to take as when we are reaching out to another person and discussing our relationship; it just might save our lives. Emotional and physical abuse can be a difficult attribute in a relationship to identify. If we don't have a lot of experience with relationships, initially the situation can become quite confusing and cause a lot of distress.

If you are in a manipulating situation, where the partner is trying to convince you that the relationship is something worth holding onto, however in reality it is not, then talking to someone else may help you sort out your own thoughts and gain clarity.

That is the whole point on justified complaining: we are not essentially seeking someone to make a decision for us. We are not seeking just attention from other people or trying to create a drama that doesn't really exist. Justified complaining means that we have a reason to seek a trustworthy ear that will listen to us and allow us the comfort of sharing our personal experience with them.

So when you find that you are complaining about something due to your own dissatisfaction you need to ask yourself, why are you unhappy? Sometimes it can just be a matter of our attitudes that particular day. Maybe we are frustrated with ourselves and it is reflecting onto other areas of our lives. It is important to allow yourself time to see if your perspectives have changed after a day or two. If you are still feeling the same way and are feeling overwhelmed or burdened by the issue, then the complaint alone has escalated to a discomfort and unhappiness.

If you have recently made a rather large change in your life and are still uncertain about the change that you made, allow yourself 3-6 months to decide whether or not the change was beneficial or something you were just using in the interim. You want to give yourself time to acclimate to a situation. You may find that after 3-6 months you feel more comfortable and are glad that you hung in there and overcame your own indecisiveness. Or just the opposite can occur and you find that after this time, you are still not satisfied with the situation and need to seek something you feel is rewarding and beneficial.

So when you are writing in your journal on your dissatisfactions make sure you set a plan for action. Give yourself a time frame that you are allowing yourself to make a decision or your next course of action, and most importantly stick to it. If you are dissatisfied now and then find out 6 months from now you are still unhappy, then do not continue to put yourself in your own misery. Take action.

Put effort into making changes. If it is job related, take that time to look for new opportunities. Just the mere fact that you are looking into new beginnings can help comfort you in a situation you are unhappy with.

If the actual issue is a relationship that you find you are dissatisfied with, then instead of seeking a new partner while you are with the current partner, make a commitment to yourself. Set aside some time after the relationship dissolves to be alone. Give yourself a time frame where you don't focus on dating, you focus on where your own direction is with the relationship you have with yourself.

If we don't know where we are going then it is kind of hard to take someone with us. There is nothing wrong with giving yourself some self-discovery time.

So take out your journal and reflect on moments where you have actually made justified complaints to someone. Think about how you handled the situation you were dissatisfied with after you discussed your grievances with someone else. Were you happy with the outcome or not happy? Did you feel that you were able to find a solution just by discussing your feelings with someone? How many times did you feel you might have over-reacted in situations that caused more harm than good? How many times did you feel that you did not do enough in a situation?

Everything has a purpose and when we sit down and write about the events that have occurred in our lives we can begin to see areas that we have experienced growth on and areas that we want to explore further. Writing may also help you with recognizing a series of patterns that you never realized before.

Be willing and be open to discover yourself and the intricate details on your own happiness. Our whole goal is to create such an abundance of happiness that we have lessened our complaining to only that which is justified versus complaining simply for the usage of our time.

Journal Exercise 9

1. So take out your journal and reflect on moments where you have actually made justified complaints to someone. Think about how you handled the situation you were dissatisfied with after you discussed your grievances with someone else. Were you happy with the outcome or not happy? Did you feel that you were able to find a solution just by discussing your feelings with someone? How many times did you feel you might have over reacted in situations that caused more harm than good? How many times did you feel that you did not do enough in a situation?

2. Are you seeing any patterns now that you have your thoughts written down? If so, what were they and what can you do to avoid or change the outcome?

Chapter 10

taking ACTION

Do not spend time complaining about something you have the power to change. If you see that something needs to be done, then do it. Don't just wait for someone else to take the initiative to recognize your complaint and take action. Instead gain the satisfaction of knowing that you set out to accomplish something you felt that needed to be done.

Don't wait for other people to recognize the same details and intricacies that you recognize. If you see something you want to change and you have the power to do so then by all means get up and do it. Don't waste a breath just sitting there talking about what should be done. Instead just get up and do it.

Your goal should be to complain less and do more. Instead of putting something off that you know needs to be done, just take the time you spend complaining about something and instead get the task done. Instead of procrastination, try motivation.

What ultimately occurs when a person procrastinates is that they keep putting off various daily tasks in their lives that require their action and presence to the point where they become overwhelmed by the amount of things they need to do. And instead of taking any action at all they become frozen. They can no longer see a clear starting point and a clear ending point. So they have no idea where to begin.

So they allow things to accrue until they no longer can tolerate it and then they are forced to do something, to take some sort of action. This can be in regards to any daily life function. You can have two people paying their monthly bills and both people would pay them differently. One person might pay the bill right away to avoid feeling a burden at the end of the month. The other person might wait right until the actual due date to pay their bills. One person is alleviating unnecessary stress and the other one is right on the edge giving themselves a lot of opportunity to forget their responsibility or be late on their payment.

Set realistic and obtainable goals. Set goals that you can accomplish. Start out small and work your way up to the larger-scaled goals. When we say starting out small, try making small changes or goals. Maybe you have a day where you are going to actually focus on how many times you complain in one 24-hour period. Your goal could be to keep it under 10 complaints. Then all day you practice obtaining this goal.

You could focus on small goals like eating healthy. Just focus on one day: not tomorrow, not next week, or a month from now. Narrow your focus down to this moment and this day. You don't want to overwhelm yourself with unnecessary clutter. You have control over today; you don't have any control over what happens tomorrow or next week.

Some people like making themselves lists. They feel more focused if they have a list that tells what they are supposed to accomplish and what goals they want to obtain. So if that works for you, by all means do it. It is a simple way to keep yourself organized. The less clutter in your mental arena the better. You are in charge of keeping your mental clarity tidy. It is hard to take any form of action on even the most simple of tasks, if your head is filled with clutter.

A perfect example is when you are trying to focus on something, but your mind is elsewhere. You want to focus on your work, but thinking of something else hinders you. Everyone can become preoccupied with his or her life. This is only natural, but you can become engulfed by your own thoughts and chaos. If you keep yourself focused on accomplishing one goal at a time then you will not become overwhelmed and place a burden on yourself that could induce complaining.

We will never fully be able to eliminate complaining altogether but we will hopefully be able to reduce it tremendously by creating an environment that we feel accomplished with instead of smothered by. Throughout the book you were asked to take several assessments of your daily dissatisfactions. Now we want you to take time to write about the actions you are going to take going forward.

What obtainable goals can you accomplish right now? What short-term goals do you want to accomplish? What forms of action are you going to take to create a more positive living environment for yourself? What changes are you going to invoke?

Remember your body and your mind work together. They are constantly trying to get you on the right path to where everything can function properly. If you are unhappy, your body is going to provide you with signals to alert you. Sickness will be present. If you are happy your body seems to overcome illness. So focus in on what your intuitions have been telling you. If something feels wrong then it generally is and you have to work towards remedying the issue so that you can obtain peace of mind.

What we just said in a sentence or two can take someone months or even years to accomplish if they are not actively listening to the hints their body and mind are providing them with. If you are making a major life change then taking time out to think the situation through is essential.

Write down your actions. Don't worry about censoring yourself when you are writing your thoughts either. Don't worry about imperfections here; this is all for you. You are writing down your goals so that you can see them. Sometimes we need to lay everything out in the open for ourselves to see more clearly. Remember this helps us organize our thoughts and see the actions that we want to take right in front of our eyes. Basically you are laying a map down and seeing how you can get from point A to point B.

We started out by writing about where we are currently and now we are writing about where we want to be. Once you have completed this process, try to set an actual date of completion. Give yourself a deadline. Some people work better under pressure of having a date to go off of so it is helpful to give yourself a timeframe to complete the tasks you intended.

This will only work if you stick to the date. Don't make any excuses for yourself. You may actually work your schedule so that you can accomplish this goal and make something important to you a priority.

After you have accomplished some of your goals, go back and reread your journal notes. This is a great reminder for you to know where you were when you started. Evaluate your life now. Do you see improvements? What changes have you made? Are you sticking to some of the goals you set out to accomplish?

Most importantly, are you complaining less? Are you more satisfied with your life now after taking these actions? How have your views of others changed in the making of this process? Have the people you choose to be around changed or did you change being around them?

Little changes can go a long way. They give us a sense of control in situations that we don't realize that we have options or choices. It reinstates our independence. It gives us hope for a new day and a new tomorrow. We find that we can start over any time we choose to. We do have the right to be happy. We have the right to enjoy our life instead of just complain about it.

The changes you make will impact others as well and perhaps you will become an example to those who feel they are at a similar junction in their lives. Your attitude, your gratification, and your response to those around you will reflect onto others. So be mindful of your words, your thoughts, and your notions.

Shed light on a situation instead of darkness. View changes as necessary instead of pointless. Accept life as is and not guaranteed. Smile even if it hurts to. Laugh. Live. And say "thank you" every chance you get as this is an opportunity for you to show how grateful you are for what you have right now.

Journal Exercise 10

1. What obtainable goals can you accomplish right now? What short-term goals do you want to accomplish? What forms of action are you going to take to create a more positive living environment for yourself? What changes are you going to invoke?

2. We started out by writing about where we are currently and now we are writing about where we want to be. Once you have completed this process try to set an actual date of completion. Give yourself a deadline. Some people work better under pressure of having a date to go off of so it is helpful to give yourself a timeframe to complete the tasks you intended.

3. After you have accomplished some of your goals go back and reread your journal notes. This is a great reminder for you to know where you were when you started. Evaluate your life now. Do you see improvements? What changes have you made? Are you sticking to some of the goals you set out to accomplish?

4. Most importantly, are you complaining less? Are you more satisfied with your life now after taking these actions? How have your views of others changed in the making of this process? Have the people you choose to be around changed or did you change being around them?

Printed in Great Britain
by Amazon.co.uk, Ltd.,
Marston Gate.